AFRICA *2001*

Other books by Herbert Ekwe-Ekwe

Conflict and Intervention in Africa (Macmillan, 1990)

The Biafra War, Nigeria and the Aftermath (Edwin Mellen, 1990)

Issues in Nigerian Politics Since the Fall of the Second Republic 1984-1990 (Edwin Mellen, 1991)

AFRICA *2001*

The State, Human Rights and the People

Herbert Ekwe-Ekwe

International Institute for Black Research
READING

First published 1993

Published by

The INTERNATIONAL INSTITUTE FOR BLACK RESEARCH
34-36 Crown Street, Reading, Berks RG1 2SE, England

Printed by: The QWERTY PRESS Ltd, Reading, Berks RG3 2RA

British Library Cataloguing in Publication Data
Ekwe-Ekwe, Herbert
Africa 2001: The State, Human Rights and the People

1. Africa, African World - History and Politics
I. Title

ISBN 1-874387-01-X

FOR

Christopher Okigbo

Booker Little   Lee Morgan
Paul Chambers   Art Blakey

Onwuka Dike

There was bitterness. There was anger over the years of suffering. The centuries of atrocities continued...   This anger was appropriate, a sign of being alive, thinking, and at our best. The music spoke of kindness, beauty, the creator and humanistic values. This was us at our most creative for when an oppressed people are quiet, they are not creative. They are walking dead.

- Cuthbert Simpkins, *Coltrane: A Bibliography*
(Baltimore: Black Classics, 1989)

CONTENTS

Acknowledgements

I wish to thank Annie Martin for commenting valuably on the manuscript of this book, and Sully Abu, Nii K. Bentsi-Enchill, Michael 'Muce' Ejieh, Elom ('Chief of Staff') Dovlo, Ndubisi Eke, Onwuchekwa Jemie, David Johnson, Xolani Mkhanazi, Chike Obidigbo, Amma Ogan, and Lemmy Owugah for the most fruitful and engaging discussions on the history and politics of the African World. I am very grateful to computer experts Kevin Haywood, Davis James, Beverley Joseph and Tony Williams for their prompt search and successful rescue of several pages of the manuscript that suddenly went 'missing' from the computer disk on which I was working on Christmas eve last year. Their brotherly and sisterly intervention prevented what would have been a damaging delay in the completion of this book. Thank you all. For their most loving support, thanks are due to my parents Humphrey and Gladys Ekwe-Ekwe, and Helen, Ngozi, Uchendu, Amechi, Chima, Chinyere and Esther.

Herbert Ekwe-Ekwe, London, 17 March 1993

To overhaul a history, or attempt to redeem it - which effort may or may not justify it - is not at all the same thing as the descent one must make in order to excavate a history. To be forced to excavate a history is, also, to repudiate the concept of history, and the vocabulary in which history is written; for the written history is, and must be, merely the vocabulary of power, and power is history's most seductively attired false witness. And yet, the attempt, more, the necessity, to excavate a history, to find out the truth about oneself! is motivated by the need to have the power to force others to recognise your presence, your right to be here. The disputed passage will remain disputed so long as you do not have the authority of the right-of-way - so long, that is, as your passage can be disputed: the document promising safe passage can always be revoked. Power clears the passage, swiftly: but the paradox, here, is that power, rooted in history, is also, the mockery and the repudiation of history. The power to define the other seals one's definition of oneself - who, then, in such a fearful mathematic... is trapped?

- James Baldwin, *Just Above My Head* (Corgi Books,1980)

Chapter 1

The Long Haul: The Trajectory to the Restoration of Independence

Whenever it occurred, Africa's independence, or more historically correct, the *re-establishment* of Africa's independence after 500 years of European imperialism, was sure to be a turning point in the history of African peoples. It would be the beginning of an extensive re-construction process for a continent which had for a greater part of a millennium been the target of a ruthless and devastating trail of invasions, murders, mass exportations of its peoples, occupations and subjugation first by Arab/muslim armies from western Asia beginning in the 7th century, and later on by Europeans in the 15th century. These invasions and occupations represent the second and third 'seasons'[1] respectively of the Euro-Asian conquest of Africa, with the first 'season' which lasted for 12 centuries (525 BC to the beginning of the 7th century AD), and which was characterised principally by the seizure and colonisation of north Africa (one-third of the continent's territory), from the north-west Atlantic coast, to the Red Sea in the east. It was during the first season of conquest that the great African civilisation of Egypt, humanity's first recorded civilisation, was overrun and occupied first by the Persians, then the Greeks, and later the Romans, as well as the expanded Roman occupation of the other African civilisations west of Egypt.[2]

The Great Relay Race - The Arab/muslim Baton

The 7th century Arab/muslim seizure of north Africa, and the subsequent invasions of the west African kingdom of Ghana by the Almoravids, a muslim expeditionary force from western Sahara, accelerated the simultaneous islamisation/Arabisation and de-Africanisation of the cultural heritage of Sahelian west Africa, as evident in the legacies left behind by a number of influential kingdoms and empires which flourished in this region between the 10th and 16th century, most notably Mali, Songhai and Kanem Bornu. The islamisation of the leadership and the key institutions of these states, a process which began most unremittingly in Kanem in the 11th century, and later acquired a profound galvinisation in Mali and Songhai, accentuated the de-Africanisation of the Sahel. Soon, these leaderships would begin to construct bogus genealogies linking themselves and their forebears to the family tree of the founder of the islamic religion

1

in Arabia,[3] a tendency that is still much in vogue in contemporary islamised Africa: 'All the royal families, without distinction, after islamization invented Sherifian origin for themselves, often retroactively adjusting local history... Such legends have proliferated in Africa... and have contributed to altering the authentic history of the continent... [The] consciousness of the continuity of the people's historical past has [thus] been progressively weakened by religious influences.'[4] A tragic feature of this pulverisation of African history is found presently in the Sudan where islamised Africans who are historically descended from the ancient Nubian kingdom of Meroe show no enthusiasm in identifying themselves openly with this illustrious pre-islamic past: 'The ruins from the period, the eighty-four pyramids still standing in the ancient capital, the temple of Semna, Meroitic writing, the remains of the astronomical observatories, the vestiges of the metal industry which made the Sudan the Birmingham of antiquity, all this is of no interest because it is tainted with a pagan tradition no good muslim would think of recalling...'[5] On the broader compass of contemporary African historiography, there exists despite 1200 years of Arab/muslims enslaving, conquest and plunder of Africa, an insidious politico-intellectual orthodoxy among some African scholars, particularly those who are muslim, to corral into a cocoon of 'defensiveness' when faced with the subject of the African World - Arab/muslim relations. This has often ranged from the proselytising genre of a Mazrui,[6] through the apologia of a Niane,[7] to the extremely unusual uncriticalness of a Diop[8]. As historian and literary critic Chinweizu has forcefully shown,[9] this orthodoxy has had four grave effects on our understanding of Africa's history during this epoch: (a) it attempts to 'minimise the role of war in the spread of Islam in Africa'; (b) it refuses to see 'Islamisation as a cover for cultural, and sometimes biological Arabisation - as imposition of Arab language, culture, religion, laws, customs and *even rulers on African populations'* (emphasis added); (c) it 'refuses to probe the role of White racism in the Afro-Arab encounter,' and (d), it 'fails to present a focused view of the price Africans paid for Islamisation.'

Elsewhere in society, to return to our discussion of the Sahelian west African empires, we observe that their leaderships' 'preoccupation to identify fully with the cultural and religious dictates of Arabia and the Arab World, was carried out with utmost zest. The ostentatiousness that surrounded especially the religious pilgrimages to Mecca by the ruling *Mansa* or *Askia* or *Sunni* or *Uthman* of the day was a dramatic feature of the gratuitous transfer of Africa's wealth abroad, the hallmark of these 'seasons' of foreign conquest and occupation. 'When the most powerful of the emperor of Mali [Mansa Musa] passed through Cairo on pilgrimage to Mecca in the fourteenth century, he ruined the price of the Egyptian gold-based dinar for several years by his presents and payments of unminted gold to couriers and merchants.'[10] A century later, whilst on his own pilgrimage to Mecca, Askia Mohammed of Songhai travelled with '300,000 gold pieces... Upon his arrival, he gave 100,000 as alms to the cities of Mecca and Medina and purchased in Medina a mansion which was to serve as a hostel for pilgrims from the Sudan. This mansion must have been large, for the cost of maintenance came to 100,000 gold pieces.'[11] Six hundred years later, there is still no let up in this form of dissipation of African wealth. In contemporary Nigeria, for example, the muslim pilgrimage to Mecca costs the country 'some one hundred million naira yearly in foreign exchange that is not infrequently invested in smuggling of drugs, gold bars, electronics... lace material.'[12]

Retrogression

This Arab/muslim hegemony easily encrusted onto the foundations of these feudal states of Sahelian African an Asiatic retrograde patriarchal system which still oppresses and dehumanises African womanhood. This system, which would be reinforced later in Africa by comparable features of the judeo-christian patriarchal heritage of the Indo-European World, is in contradistinction to the African matriarchal system which had flourished for centuries, particularly in the anti-state principalities of the continent.[13] The African matriarchy encapsulates the totality of social existence. In the classic Igbo example,[14] it possesses a flexible gender system which enables men and women to share their *access* to economic resources and institutions of social and political authority democratically. This matriarchy has developed agelong 'checks and balances' and a 'moral system which generate[s] the concepts of love, harmony and co-operation... and [thus] impose[s] a check on excessive and destructive masculinism.'[15] So, in this system, women are able to operate unhindered in institutions which organise and control 'agricultural work, trade, the markets, and women's culture and its relevant ideology.'[16] As Ifi Amadiume has aptly demonstrated, the power enjoyed by African women in the continent's matriarchal system, unlike the current powerlessness, marginalisation and commoditisation of women in the localised Euro-Asian patriarchal model, had an 'economic and ideological basis [in society] which derived from the importance accorded to motherhood.'[17]

Besides the introduction of a brutish Asiatic patriarchy, the Arab/ muslims converted their north African occupation, and cultural hegemony in Sahelian west Africa into a profitable conurbation for the enslavement and export of Africans as slaves, as well as other resources such as gold particularly, to the Arab World, Asia, and southern Europe. At the height of the occupation, the Arab/muslims exported two million Africans per annum as slaves to the Arab World,[18] and extensively depleted the gold reserves in the Sudan, Mali, Songhai, Kanem-Bornu and elsewhere, which were transferred to enrich the bourses and palaces of the Arab world. Considering the magnitude of this export of African resources at the time, it is not without significance that the Arabs themselves have a saying: 'Against the camel's mange use tar, and against poverty make a trip to the Sudan.'[19]

The role of the Arab world *itself* in the re-export of the slaves in its territory to southern Europe (in addition to the Near-East and south-west Asia) during the period - a practice which dramatically doubled and in some cases tripled the value of the slaves - was such that in Naples, for example, 83 per cent of the slaves there by the 15th century were Africans.[20] And, contrary to 'conventional' wisdom, African slaves worked Arab/muslim sugar plantations in Morocco as early as the 9th century, almost 600 years before the Americas! Morocco itself would later on in 1593 attack, pillage, and seize prominent towns of Songhai, leading ultimately in its wake to the collapse of the Songhai empire, ironically the most islamised of the Sahelian west African states.

Parallel to these events in west Africa, Arab/muslim expansionism in east Africa, subsequent to the initial 7th century incursion of Africa, soon spread along the Somali, Kenyan and Mozambican coastline, and their occupation of the off-shore island of Zanzibar which they later transformed into a strategic slave colony. From these coastal bridgeheads the Arabs began to exert enormous influence into the affairs of the existing independent states and principalities of the African hinterland - in the east, east-central, central and southern Africa. In the latter two regions, as were the cases in north and western Africa, they pursued a scorched earth programme of brigandage, murders and the enslavement and export of millions of African peoples to the Arab World and elsewhere, a practice that actively went on well into the 16th century when *it*, in turn, was enveloped by the burgeoning Europe's eventual take-over of Africa. The Zulu chronicler, Vusamazulu Credo Mutwa recalls most chillingly the aftermath of the Arab slave trade in southern Africa: 'Our historians mentioned that no less than a hundred [nations and nationalities] were wiped out completely in Tanganyika, Kenya, the Congo basin and [Zambia].'[21] Finally, in east-central Africa in the early 1500s, the Arab/muslims dealt a further blow to Africa's independence. They overran the three successor states of Nubia, essentially the surviving bastions of Africa's ancient Nile valley civilisations, thus extending their territorial stranglehold on the Nile further south to the river's strategic middle stretches.

As we have just shown, the cataclysmic entrails of the export of African peoples as slaves, and the plunder of their natural resources, two *crucial* features that would underline the European invasion of Africa as from the 15th century, were indeed fully operationalised with devastating effects by the Arab/muslim occupation of the continent much earlier. In this context, the Arab/muslim invasion directly paved the way to Europe's subsequent attack. Chancellor Williams, the eminent African American historian has observed:[22]

> As Arabisation spread among [the Africans] so did slavery and the slave raiding. The Arabs' insatiable and perpetual demands for slaves had long since changed slavery from an institution that signalled a military victory by the number of captured prisoners, to an institution that provided warfare expressly for the enslavement of men, women, and children for sale and resale. Human beings had now openly become very profitable articles for trade and slave dealers had found shorter routes to quicker riches.

For Africa, therefore, the first phase of this holocaust of a millennium was now under way, and Europe would attempt to push this process to a final solution, starting from the 15th century.

The Great Relay Race - Europe takes over

Within 300 years of achieving the strategic control of Africa's resources (human and natural), Europe would lay the foundation for the West's political and economic hegemony of the contemporary world. Britain, the first truly effective Western global power, used the gargantuan capital it accumulated during its African slave trade to finance its so-called industrial revolution, the turning point in the development of Western capitalism.

Britain's success on this score cannot be over-stressed. This was a country which prior to the mid-17th century was still a 'cultural and scientific backwater,' to borrow the graphic description made by Christopher Hill, the well-known British historian whose scholarship specialises on this period.[23] By the beginning of the 18th century however, Britain had established virtual world monopoly of the African slave trade (in a comparative study of the 'worth' of the African slave and that of the labour of an English worker then, the economist Charles Davenant in the late 17th century noted: '[The labour of a slave in the West Indies] is worth six times as much as the labour of an Englishman at home'[24]) and used the enormous resources that accrued to it to finance its burgeoning scientific and technological enterprises. Britain soon became the 'centre of world science.'[25] For the Western World as a whole, the capital generated from its African slave trade was the basis on which its capitalism was largely built,[26] a point poignantly made in a major study by the French economist Michel Beaud who reminds the European World: 'We should never forget that this [the African slave trade] was an essential basis (though largely erased and ignored in Western thought) for the [Western] enrichment of the sixteenth, seventeenth and eighteenth centuries.'[27]

The effect on the African of this latest holocaust, as should be expected, was devastating as the active human power of millions of future generations were uprooted and shipped off to the Americas by European slavers to work the tobacco, sugar and cotton plantations, and excavate the gold and silver mines in these territories that had just been conquered by a rampaging European imperialism. Africa lost one hundred to three hundred million of its peoples as slaves during the period, including those who died whilst on the overland journey to slave ships and the passage to the Americas.[28] Its society was weakened and in turmoil, and was soon subjected to another emergency from Europe, as the latter determined how best to utilise the remaining African population and the continent's rich land (and sea) resources for the continuing service of their economies - historically formalised by the occupation of most of Africa by Britain, France, Germany, Italy, Belgium, Spain and Portugal beginning in the latter part of the 19th century. Soon, Africa was turned into a reservoir of cheap labour for intensive and extensive agricultural and mineralogical exploitation necessitated by the occupation. The African farmer was converted overnight into a cash 'crop farmer', a term of dubious meaning, but essentially cultivating assorted crops such as palm produce, cotton, cocoa, groundnut, sisal and cloves solely for export to European markets. Alternatively,

African labour was deployed to the ever-expanding European mining corporations dotted all over the continent to extract various types of minerals including gold, diamonds, tin, bauxite, iron ore, coal, and copper, and petroleum products, again for export to Europe. In effect African land and property relations, which in most cases were characterised by an agelong system of communitarianism, were abolished to make way for private appropriation of land for both plantation agriculture and mining enterprises already referred to, or for the construction of new communication infrastructure, or for *direct* settlement of European immigrants as exemplified in parts of north Africa (Algeria especially), east/southern Africa (Kenya, Tanzania, Mozambique, Zimbabwe, South Africa, Angola, Namibia) central Africa (Congo, Zaire), and west Africa (Sao Tomé, Equatorial Guinea, Gabon, Cameroon, Côte d'Ivoire, Senegal, Guinea-Bissau, Cape Verde). In each conquered territory, now arbitrarily carved out from hitherto existing African states and principalities, the imperial regime imposed its own monetary system on society and also ensured that the terms for the exchange of goods and services, *fundamental for the logical development of any socioeconomic activity or relation,* was inextricably tailored to the exigencies of the home market back in Europe. All forms of taxes were imposed to expedite this European take-over of Africa, and the strategic spheres of the continent's pre-colonial culture, industrial, and other forms of technological creativity therein were curtailed or suppressed. No doubt, the economies that emerged subsequently in Africa, particularly on the eve of the re-establishment of the peoples' independence in the 1960s, were structurally bereft of local needs and priorities. Instead, these were mineralogical and agricultural redoubts to service a rapacious European home market, and, at the same time, acted as conduits for European immigration.

In summary, two distinct consequences on the African humanity can be discerned from the European conquest: (a) the destruction/near-destruction of local populations (genocide), and the herding of survivors/others into labour reserves/'town ships' to make way for direct European occupation (particularly east/southern Africa), and (b) the overall control of subjugated populations, and the conversion of human and natural resources to serve imperial interests (the rest of Africa).

Contours of Resistance

The above overview of Africa's historical legacy of the past millennium, with its emphasis on the cataclysmic furloughs of foreign conquests and occupations, inevitably raises the fundamental question of African response. Indeed, a criticism that could be made on a review that accentuates the travails of foreign aggression on a people during a long expanse of human history such as a millennium, is that it paints a picture so overwhelming in its profile of a society under siege, with apparently limited space made available, simultaneously, to comprehend how the people were responding to the emergency. The point though was that the conquest of Africa by these hordes of extra-continental forces and interests did not occur in a swoop! As a result, African responses, and here we are really talking of African resistance, was essentially variegated both in time and space and would therefore require a completely separate canvass of sketches as counterpoint to the former!

African peoples were never some stupefied sitting ducks awaiting wearily for the next invasion by a foreign military contingent. On the contrary, the African landscape was saturated by multifaceted strands of communities of resistance. Several of the states, nations and nationalities contiguous to the empires of islamised Sahelian west Africa, particularly the Mossi, Cayor, Gwari, Birom and Tiv were admirably resilient in mounting and sustaining the defence of their homelands from being overrun by muslim forces for centuries. Indeed the Mossi and Cayor each retained for about two thousand years, autogenous, unadulterated African state systems with fully entrenched constitutions.[29] In effect both states predated the islamic empires of the region. They effectively coexisted with them, having held the latter at bay from overrunning their countries especially during the apogee of the islamic proselytising territorial expansionism of Songhai under Askia Mohammed in the late 15th century/ early 16th century. This ancient independence legacy was however dented slightly in the case of Cayor when one of its most influential kings in the 19th century embraced islam. But as Cheikh Anta Diop, the distinguished Afrocentric scholar has argued, this conversion was for 'diplomatic reasons,'[30] as this king, Latdjor Diop, was keen to construct a pan-African coalition of military forces in the region, aimed at incorporating, among others, islamised peoples in Salum and Trarzas, to oppose the ever-threatening French imperialist army of General Faidherbe. Even then, an islamised Cayorian aristocratic grouping, the Domi Sokhna, were held in contempt by their 'blood' brothers who constituted another branch of the nobility, but who still upheld the worship of African traditional religions, and respect for its cosmogony.[31] Taking cognisance of the matriarchy of social existence in Cayor, the latter sought, through an ingenious, albeit dramatic effort, to restrict the islamic influence of the Domi Sokhna in the state, or as they had put it, 'limit (sic) the damage done,'[32] by literally kidnapping the daughters of the Domi Sokhna (!) and then arrange for their marriage to members of the non-islamised Tieddos - state officials which included courtiers and soldiers.

African resistance against expansionist islamisation also occurred in the most unlikely of constituencies during the period - in the royal courts of islamised states! In Songhai, for instance (which was to emerge as the most islamised of the Sahelian states after Askia Mohammed became emperor in 1493), Baro, the son and would-be successor of the influential emperor, Sonni Ali, renounced islam completely, extending in effect the latter's publicly-acknowledged agnosticism towards islam which was evident throughout his reign. Subsequently, Ali's career was vilified in the accounts of a leading islamic chronicler of the day who was also very critical of the emperor's robust counter-military attacks against a (muslim) Tuareg expeditionary force which had earlier occupied some Songhai territory. During the fighting, which led to Ali's crushing defeat of the Tuareg, some islamic scholars resident in Songhai were massacred for 'collaborating' with the Tuareg, a development which no doubt alienated Ali further from his islamic critic(s). Earlier on in his career, Ali had followed in the foot steps of some of his predecessors in joining a radical independent islamic sect which did not recognise any supreme order that exercised authority over the entire muslim world, and that also felt that given the appropriate capabilities, anybody in the kingdom could achieve the highest office in the land (emperor) irrespective of their socioeconomic background.[33]

Thus generally considered, these African leaderships of the islamised states of the Sahel were extremely cautious, if not ambivalent about how to get on with practising their newly acquired religion from Arabia. While reasons for the caution would differ from empire to empire, and also from one epoch to another (say, within a given empire), the question of legitimacy must have been prominent, especially when this new faith still had to contend fiercely with the African religious and cosmogonic heritage deeply embedded in the sensibilities of the population at large. This would account for the quite unusual practice of many an emperor, king or state functionary who would sneak into the sanctuary of an African traditional religious priest, receive prayers and blessings, particularly during an acute crisis in society, even whilst working in a state whose 'official' religion was islam. In essence, Africa's ancient religious order became the last defensive and perhaps the most resilient outpost for the peoples' resistance against Arab/ muslim conquest. Africa would soon have to tap into this resource, and others in its armoury, as it responded to another emergency that threatened its independence - this time from Europe, beginning from the 15th century.

Africa's resistance to European imperialism is a subject that has been extensively researched upon and published in a library of books, journals and other publications in the past 40 years by African historians and social scientists. What follows here is pointedly an *aide-mémoire*, highlighting the dominant forms that resistance took during the course of Europe's aggression and its subsequent occupation of the continent.

There were nine principal spheres in which African resistance was organised:[34] (a) total armed struggle; (b) the independent African churches (reminiscent, in some sense, of the independent muslim sects of former epochs); (c) cultural/welfare organisations within constituent nations and nationalities (now arbitrarily constituted in the new states created by the occupation regime); (d) crop-hold ups/switches to new crop production by small-scale farmers; (e) competing for commercial territories exclusively earmarked for European business interests; (f) tax evasions/boycotts; (g) campaigns against imposition of imperial (European) currency on society; (h) strikes by wage-earners working in plantations and mines, and finally (i) sporadic revolts/uprisings (often classified as 'riots' or 'rebellions' in colonial historiography). Depending on which epoch in a given society is considered, any of the above methods, or a combination of some, would usually be the most prominent form of resistance, with the totalising universe of Africa's religious heritage providing the spiritual base for the defence.

Armed struggle, expectedly, was the most featured element of Africa's initial defence of its homeland. The African historical landscape is extensively and indelibly marked by the peoples' heroism during this defence, a heroism made more pronounced considering the all too well known superiority of the firearms deployed by the invaders as was evident in some of the most outstanding military confrontations of the era: Benin... Ijebu(Yorubaland)... Igbo... Niger Delta... Nupe... Hausa-Fulani states... Dahomey... Asante... Senegambian states... Sierra Leone Dwelling Tax War... Mossi... Kenedougou... Bambara... Mandingo... Baule... Chokwe... Bihe... Ganguela... Yaka... Bowa... Budja... Chikunda... Humbe... Cuamato... Ovimbundu... Lunda... Chewa... Herero... Zulu... Ndebele... Bemba...

Shona... Quitanghona... Makua-Swahili coalition... Yao... Makonde... Hehe... Nandi... Bunyoro... Sudan... Ethiopia...

Apart from Ethiopia where the Africans routed the invading Italian colonial army in 1895 and thus safeguarded their independence, Europe ultimately won these wars by the first decade of the 20th century largely for the reason already stated, but it should be stressed that the African resistance was victorious in a number of epic battles fought during the course of these conflicts as the following examples illustrate: the 1824 Asante defeat of the British army; the 1879 Zulu defeat of another contingent of British forces; the 1891 Hehe defeat of German forces in south-east Africa (contemporary Tanzania), and the celebrated defeat, in 1904, of the Portuguese military by a combined force of the Humbe and Cuamato in a famous battle in southern Angola. Subsequently, as Europe started to consolidate the new states it was creating out of its conquest, African resistance would begin to take new dimensions - away from the open or frontal armed response, with its 'inevitable defeat... too obviously suicidal,'[35] as C.L.R. James, a leading philosopher of the pan-African liberation struggle would sensitively describe it later, to focus, usually more eclectically, on the rest of other spheres of defence referred to earlier.

Consolidation

The principal site at which Europe embarked on the consolidation of its African conquest was of course the burgeoning colonial economy. This was facilitated by the construction or expansion of communication infrastructure such as roads, railways, waterways, ports and telegraph. These served three immediate purposes: (a) used as launching pads for more military aggression against the people, especially those in outlying districts still resisting expanding colonial 'order'; (b) helped to increase the mobility of occupying military/security/administrative personnel around territory of acquisition, and, in some cases, into contiguous territory that the colonial power also laid claim to; (c) arterial connections from ports or strategic entrepôts to parts of territory where major agricultural (palm oil, coffee, rubber, cotton, sisal, cocoa, groundnut, etc) and/or mineralogical (gold, diamond, coal, tin, bauxite) exploitation were under way.

The success of Europe's conquest of Africa coincided with a period of a major shortage of tropical agricultural products required for both human consumption and industry in the Northern World. This had been triggered off by a boom in economic activity as from 1900 (leading up to the eve of the First World War in 1914), a follow-up to the debilitating recession of the previous decade.[36] So, for Europe, its recent formal take-over of Africa could not have occurred at a more auspicious moment: '... Since these areas were now under direct European control, the largest part of the profits of this expansion could be diverted into European hands either by direct ownership of the agricultural domains, by monopolistic control of the purchasing of the product for export, by monopolistic control of transportation facilities, or by direct taxation.'[37]

The whole process of the imperialist power's introduction and development of these agricultural commodities (or 'cash crops' as Europe would soon begin to describe the products) in a given colony was essentially arbitrary and haphazard, as the goal was clearly to maximise the profits targeted with little or no consideration of the relationship and impact of this sector of activity to the rest of the economy. The resultant effect of this strategy of exploitation was the creation in Africa of specific-purpose mono-cultural, or at best (?) dual-cultural economies whose basis of existence was essentially dictated by European needs, a legacy that would plague the African inheritance subsequently but particularly after the restoration of independence as we shall show later in this study. Britain had by 1911 converted a country such as Ghana (then the British Gold Coast) into the world's largest cocoa producer, and on the eve of the Second World War in 1939, cocoa's share of Ghana's total trade was approximately 80 per cent.[38] Prior to this development, Ghana's main agricultural export concentrated on palm oil and palm kernels. In Gambia, another British colony, the shift from a main focus on the production of hides and beeswax (at one stage, accounting for 90 per cent of the country's export) to groundnut was such that within a period of about 50 years, the latter took over the role of the former as the principal export crop,[39] and within a century accounted for nearly 100 per cent of total Gambian export trade.[40] Also on the eve of World War II, Sudan, another British colony and a typical mono-cultural economy, depended on cotton for about two-thirds of its total export product, and this increased further by 10 per cent during the course of the following decade.[41]

Even in those few countries where some diversification of commodities exploited was embarked upon, the choice of products unmistakably *underscored* the needs and priorities of the imperial market. In Sierra Leone, another British colony, palm-kernel, diamonds and iron-ore accounted for such a 'diversification', as these represented the country's principal products for export on the eve of World War II,[42] while in the federation of Rhodesia and Nyasaland (contemporary Zambia, Zimbabwe and Malawi), another British colony, the mining of copper and the farming of tobacco, again geared to the export market, marked the limits of 'diversification'. In Nigeria, yet another British colony and one of the most 'diversified' of the colonial economies in Africa, the following commodities accounted for nearly 90 per cent of the country's export products prior to the outbreak of the Second World War: rubber, cocoa, cotton, groundnuts, tin, palm-oil and palm-kernels. This seemingly admirable range of Nigeria's 'diversification' had however been achieved, thanks to the sheer size of the country, stretching from the south on the Atlantic shorelines of South-Eastern west Africa to the deciduous/savannah vegetation belt of the northern hinterland bordering on the Sahel, which ensured that the colonial regime could maximally exploit the varying climatic zones across the territory in its choice of which agricultural products it wished to grow. Even then, such choices were still dictated fundamentally by the imperatives of the British economy, *and not that* of Nigeria. Fifty years later, this 'diversification' of the Nigerian economy virtually came to an end. Even though Nigeria had since become 'independent', it is acutely significant that the export product, petroleum, which displaced the basket of commodities of economic 'diversification' enumerated above, shares an equivalent quota of the country's export trade currently as the latter did a half a century earlier: 90 per cent. As should be expected, this role of petroleum has been dictated principally by the needs of British/Western economies. Whether as 'mono-cultural' or indeed 'dual-cultural', the whole logic and character of the evolving African colonial economy was to serve the interests of the imperial European occupier and, in some cases, also those of other European/Northern states.

All the examples cited above to illustrate the intrinsic nature of the colonial economy that European imperialism had begun to construct in occupied Africa as from the early decades of this century have been essentially British, but these features also apply to cases elsewhere whether these are French, Belgium, Italian, Portuguese or whatever. We have used British examples because Britain was, in the overall, the wealthiest European imperialist state in Africa with its colonies containing the majority of African peoples, the best agricultural lands, and lands saturated with an array of mineralogical products. Furthermore, on the eve of World War I, when the multifaceted gains accruing from these colonies had added to the range of prominent factors inherent in the geo-strategic calculations and priorities of many a colonial power, or indeed those of a potential one for that matter, Britain was in fact the most influential political and economic power in the world. This has led Richard Wolff to recall:[43]

> In terms of supplying food and raw material imports colonial administration meant for Britain ultimate control and hence a greater measure of security than would have obtained if France or Germany or another power had annexed the territories. Also, whatever the final destination of food and raw materials export from any colony, British political control almost always meant British predominance in the financing, insurance, and freight for the colony's exports, and hence British balance of pay-ments advantages... Colonial control enabled the British authorities to determine to a large extent the choice of foods and raw materials developed and exported from any colonial territory. Thus, it is reasonable to conclude that, *in the absence of* Britain's new empire, *her security, her gains from invisible exports, and both the general mix and quantities of food and raw materials supplied to world markets would have been less favourable to her.* (added emphasis)

Baronial Fiefdoms - I

Europe's success at converting its African colony into a haven for the growth and development of crucial raw materials required for its economy could only be done with the use of the labour of the conquered African either directly or indirectly. Essentially, this African human resource was the engine to power the construction of the haven. And as far as Europe was concerned, this key resource had to be utilised *comprehensively*, not only to ensure the success of the mission, but also to simultaneously embark on the complete dismantling of hitherto existing African political economy which still potentially acted as both a 'residual' site for continuing opposition to colonialism, and the possibilities for the restoration of independence. So, taxation became the linchpin in the colonial regime's project to utilise the African human resource for the purposes of carrying out both the construction of the requisite infrastructure, as well as the generalised processes of the exploitation of the colony's wealth. Each colony had to raise the finance to meet its administrative running costs,[44] as this was not expected from the imperial capital in Europe. Taxing the conquered Africans was therefore of utmost priority. The range of taxes paid was deliberately made as extensive as possible to incorporate both the personal and domicile facility (the so-called 'hut tax') of the adult male (even though in some circumstances colonialism extended direct taxation to the female population as was the case among the Igbo in 1929 which precipitated the famous Women's War) in society. This was aimed at facilitating the induction of the *working*-age population in the emerging colonial economy one way or the other, particularly now that the currency made legal tender was that of the occupying power's. When work was not easily available locally in some plantation, mine, or government utility establishment, or by working for one's self as a trades person, trader or farmer, the obligations to pay a myriad of colonial taxes, and also support his family, would usually drive the African male as a last resort to join the trail of migratory labour force further afield, exemplified perhaps most cogently by the notorious southern African case.[45]

Yet, for the African, the colonial taxation regime, harsh as it surely was, was only one facet in the interlocking architecture of an oppressive colonial order which the occupier effectively run as an amalgam of a fiefdom, labour camp, and a quasi-slave estate. While it has now become inevitable in any serious study of this epoch of African history to cite the unimaginable brutality to which Africans in the Congo (now Zaire) were subjected whilst the country was a personal 'property' of Belgian King Leopold II between 1885 and 1908 (a 'veritable hells-on-earth,'[46] as J. Stengers describes it), it should be stressed that this example must not be treated as an exception to a generalised trend of the atrocities and dispossession that characterised the entire colonial rule across the length and breadth of Africa. Congo was just a variation of the same kind, no doubt highlighting, usually most dramatically, similar occurrences elsewhere in the continent. It is therefore not without significance, in this context, that the wide publicity given at the time in Europe of the catalogue of maleficence perpetrated in the Congo by Leopold and his cabal of royal family often came from contending or rival imperialist interests especially those from other European states who also wanted access to the sumptuous Congo pie, as well as publicists keen to assuage estranged constituencies of 'liberal' public opinion who were now getting increasingly critical of the entire colonial enterprise in Africa.[47] In

Britain, for instance, Leopold's Congo appeared to be a favourite focus in academic and media discourses then on the 'ugly face' of European colonialism, but with the accent placed chauvinistically on what was supposed to be the alternative 'humanness' of the British experience.

Tragically for Africa, this claim was not borne out on the ground. On the contrary. Just like Leopold and other colonial potentates, the British carried out a post-conquest programme of consolidation of its rule which stretched from direct forced labour, arbitrary dispossession of peoples' lands and the encampment of victims in 'labour reserves', to the payment of grotesque wages to those offered employment. According to British colonial records in occupied Gold Coast in 1908, ironically the same year that King Leopold was forced by the Belgium government to give up his exclusive family control of the Congo partly due to the atrocities already referred to, the issue of African forced labour used in road construction in the territory had become extremely grave: 'African carriers walk[ed] constantly for a twelve month period, averaging about 400 miles a month. Naturally many of the men became incapacitated, their soles "almost completely worn through".'[48] What was the British solution to this problem? They literally *tarred* the feet of these porters.[49] And the same British records enthused over the outcome: '[This has] proved quite good and many carriers are now able to keep to the road who would otherwise have to lie up.'[50] Subsequently, for those Africans employed as civil servants in the Gold Coast, Britain paid them an average salary of £4 a month, while the average pay of a European in the same civil service was £40 a month.[51] In 1934, Britain's social services' expenditure allocation for a person living in Britain was £6 15s (six pounds, fifteen shillings).[52] In occupied Gold Coast, Britain allocated 7s 4d (seven shillings, four pence) for the same purpose, while in its colonies in Nigeria and Nyasaland, the figure was even worse at 1s 9d per individual.[53] Also in 1934, the callousness of British colonialism could not have been more illustrative in its response to the dependents of a gold mine disaster in the Gold Coast which killed forty one Africans - just the sum of £3 per victim was offered as compensation to the next-of-kin,[54] underlining most painfully what Walter Rodney means when he describes European imperialism in Africa as 'exploitation without responsibility and without redress.'[55]

Further east in its other colony in Nigeria, the British employed a combination of forced labour and the payment of 'starvation wages' to porters to carry assorted goods, particularly those meant for export, and to others involved in the frantic construction of railways, roads and telegraphic facilities that occurred especially in the first 30 years of this century. Porters were variously paid 6d to 9d per day's work, but quite often not paid at all.[56] Those who worked on the road/railway construction received 6d a day but in some of the more outlying provinces the British had paid such labour 3d per week.[57] Nigerians employed in the Enugu coal mines were paid 6d a day if they worked on the surface, and 1s per ton of coal cut if they worked underground.[58] (A note of comparison here: Whilst the appalling poverty, squalid and dangerous working environment that circumscribed the fate of the British miner during this epoch was legendary, it was nonetheless the fact that this miner was incredibly better off than his Nigerian counterpart. In Scotland, for instance, a miner, at that period, working usually in less dangerous circumstances than the miner at the Enugu colliery, was paid 1s for 1-2 hours work[59].) The workers slaved away in a punishing schedule, producing 25,000 tons of coal after the first year of mining operations in 1916, cutting dramatically the colonial regime's budgetary allocation for imported coal.[60] Such was the success of these mines that within three years, the colliery authorities not only paid for all their operations from income generated themselves, but they contributed £47,000 to the government revenue, as well as initiating corresponding savings, and later profits, in the railway department (yearly earnings here soon began to average £1 million) which no longer needed to import coal from Europe.[61] By 1945, coal output at the Enugu mines was 68,000 tons.[62] Similarly on the plateau tin fields in northern Nigeria, cheap and forced labour were the basis of another lucrative mining enterprise. In 1937, Nigerian miners there were paid a weekly average wage of 3s 6d, thus making the annual wage bill for this workforce approximately £329,000, a figure which in effect was about one quarter of the total profit of £1,249,000 made that year by the tin industry.[63] By then about 70 European business interest groups at these mines had a total capital of at least £6 million.[64]

Forced labour in Nigeria, and indeed elsewhere in British Africa, did not just end with the outright *conscription* of labour, nor the demands made on community leaders by the colonial regime to make mandatory 'allocation' of labour quotas to designated 'public works' projects, but also shared the standard track of gross de-humanisation at work place with those who 'volunteered' to work such as routine flogging by foremen/supervisors which occasionally resulted in the maiming of victims, racist verbal abuse and at times the indiscriminate shooting of workers by police or the military in the event of strikes or revolts. Equally, the arbitrary resort to the use of armed force by the regime to attack communities reluctant or seemingly unable to contribute their own quota of conscript labour was not infrequent.[65] Also not uncommon during the period, was the practice of masses of able-bodied youth simply going into long stretches of hiding, or exile from their principality, in order to escape from these essentially slave labour dispensations. Alternatively, some 'volunteered' to serve in the colonial army instead of doing forced labour elsewhere![66]

Yet, it was in eastern/southern Africa where 'settler' colonialism was more firmly in place that the British optimised most definitively the objectification and the dispossession of the African human resource. Extensive confiscation of African lands to pave way for European settlers, commercial interests, farmers, or just (land) speculators was a cardinal facet of this development. Following the seizure and the declaration of the Kenyan highlands as 'Crown Land', Britain embarked on the sale of parcels of this land at token prices to influential members of the British aristocracy and others. For a penny per acre, Lord Delamere appropriated 100,000 acres.[67] Contiguous to this estate, Lord Scott acquired 350,000 acres, while East African Syndicate and East African Estate Ltd. was each handed over 350,000 and 100,000 acres respectively elsewhere on the highlands, all at give away prices.[68] Initially, the settlers held these lands on 99-year leases, but the colonial regime subsequently extended the time limit of the leases to 999 years,[69] consequently increasing, as should be expected, the speed and acreage of appropriation, and of (European) emigration to Kenya. The Africans expelled from their lands were of course transferred to 'labour reserves' to work in the ever expanding 'cash crop' economy there or 'public works' similar to those discussed whilst we were examining the west African experience. As one Colonel Grogan, a Kenyan European settler, sardonically put it at the time, 'We have stolen his land. Now we must steal his limbs. Compulsory labour is the corollary of our occupation of the country.'[70] And to underline the historical significance of Grogan's point, the African income per capita in Kenya on the eve of the outbreak of the Mau Mau national liberation war in the early 1950s was £3.[71]

Added to these dispossession, east Africans were also subjected to another blight of alienation in their homeland. Resident Arab merchants and Asians who the British had brought to the region earlier on at the outset of colonisation as 'indentured' labour, were now, thanks to the colonial power's post-conquest programme of consolidating its rule, effectively positioned in the economies as 'middlepersons' who not only bought the 'cash crops' produced by Africans directly for re-sale to the European companies, but controlled the retail trade, and with ever more favourable credit allowances from (colonial) banks, also had some stake in the wholesale export trade. These Arabs and Asians were generally rapacious in their commercial dealings with Africans,[72] and would emerge on the morrow of the restoration of independence in the region with scant identification with the political, economic, and cultural aspirations of the countries they were domiciled. On the contrary, most took out dual British/ domiciled state nationality or outright British citizenship. With such legal guarantees, coupled with their privileged role in the economies, the Asians, particularly, succeeded in turning their east African abode into a major springboard for the steady transfer of capital to Britain and other Western countries. This success of having access to 'ready capital' abroad would later on, as from the 1960s, give Asian emigres from here who now wanted to live in Britain (or elsewhere in the West), a vital leverage in the arduous efforts to set up new homes, bring up families, and create work opportunities in their new environment, in contrast to other emigres during the period especially peoples of African descent from the Caribbean. Thus, in this regard, we should not fail to note that this entire historical legacy of Asians, from east Africa, would be mischievously ignored by certain schools of 'race relations' sociology in the Britain of the 1970s/80s bent on 'proving' what they termed the 'under achievement' of African Caribbeans in (British) society, as they dabbled in the mythologisation of the 'great Asian success' in their studies.

In Northern and Southern Rhodesia (now Zambia and Zimbabwe respectively), examples of other British 'settler colonies', the occupying regime's seizure of African lands and the incarceration of its owners into reserves, also went hand in hand with a mixture of forced and cheap labour. In the copper mines of Northern Rhodesia in the 1930s, 'unskilled' African labour was paid 7s a month.[73] African truck drivers on the mines received a wage of £3 a month while European truck drivers there, doing similar jobs, were paid £30 per month.[74] In 1937, the mines earned about £12 million from sales of copper abroad, and approximately half of this sum was paid out as dividends to share holders who lived mostly in Britain, while royalties paid to the British mine owners was £500,000.[75] For the total of 17,000 African work force here, their entire wage bill for this year was £244,000, or just about 5s 6d per individual per week.[76] In Southern Rhodesia, Africans working ten to fourteen hours a day in the municipal sectors of the economy in the 1940s were paid an average of 35s to 75s, while Europeans, employed in the same establishment, and carrying out similar tasks, received 20s for an 8-hour day work schedule in addition to the provision of free residential quarters.[77] But it was in South Africa that Britain institutionalised most horrifically the barbarism of European colonialism in Africa, and it is to this that we must now turn.

The 'Land Act' which the so-called South African Union government proclaimed in 1913 is generally cited as the legal underpinning of what later became known in South Africa as *apartheid*, or territorial 'separation' of the races. This resulted in the appropriation of 87 per cent of all lands in the country by European settlers who make up about 13 per cent of the population, and the relegation of the majority Africans to the remaining 13 per cent of territory which contains most of the squalid and unproductive lands in the country. But as historian Ronald Hyam is quick to point out, '[apartheid's] ideological and future legislative shape was first modelled by the British rather than the Afrikaners.'[78] Hyam refers to the outcome of a special study on the future of the African population in South Africa that was commissioned in 1903-5, a decade prior to the 'Land Act', by the resident British High Commissioner in the country as crucial. Godfrey Lagden, who chaired the study, was a civil servant and a director of the South African Gold Trust:

> [He] saw white supremacy as axiomatic, and race and colour as legitimate differentials in granting political rights; he saw the African as a wage labourer rather than as a peasant farmer. He envisaged an economic bar and pass laws to regulate an adequate cheap black labour force. Two features were clearly set forth in thereport. First, the principle of territorial segregation, with reserves set apart for Africans, and the racially exclusive and final delimitation of land areas. Secondly, there was to be political separation too... Not only was the [Study Commission] made up entirely of British members, the Report was received with scarcely a murmur of protest either in Britain or in South Africa.[79]

Indeed, the thinking encapsulated in the Lagden Study had already been operationalised with startling results by Britain in various chunks of territory over which it exercised control in South Africa in the previous 100 years. Whilst he was the British administrator in Natal(1845-53), and later the official principally responsible for African Affairs in the state (1853-75), Theophilus Shepstone embarked on schemes of experimentation aimed at moving African families out of their homes and lands into 'reserves', the very precursor of *apartheid*. In 1846, a Shepstone commission earmarked eight locations of approximately one million acres in total area in the Natal region for the initial 'reserve' project.[80] By 1860, Shepstone had successfully transferred 80,000 Africans into these 'reserves', and 'thus was born a system whereby Africans performed the manual work for most of the white settlers - on their farms, in their towns and villages, and in their houses - at extremely low wages.'[81] With the discovery of diamonds in 1864 and gold in 1886, Britain would convert this hostage African human resource in South Africa into a priceless strategic asset to construct its most lucrative economic stranglehold overseas. In the 1950s, British investments in South Africa stood at about £860 million with a 15 per cent annual profit yield.[82] Twenty years later, or just over a century after the first discovery of diamonds in the country, Britain's investments (direct) hit the £1 billion mark, and the annual profit margin on these increased even further to about 25 per cent, clearly placing it as the leading investor in the country.[83] And to emphasise the saliency of Britain's South African success story within the overall African perspective, we should point out that these £1 billion worth investments were, by 1975, about one-third higher than its total investment elsewhere in Africa.[84]

Britain still retains this accolade of leading investor in South Africa, and now commands total assets of awesome proportions - £12 billion.[85] This represents about one-third of all external investment here. Besides the United States and Germany, Britain is South Africa's third largest trading partner. Out of the 2000 main transnational corporations that operate in South Africa, 341 are British, second only to the United States (which has 407),[86] and these operate in the 'nerve centre' of the economy - banking, metallurgy (especially in the exploitation of key minerals such as gold, diamonds, uranium, chromium, titanium, vanadium and manganese) and communications. Until the culmination of the great African uprisings of the past two decades virtually brought the working of this economy to a screeching halt, no other country in the world was comparable to South Africa on the critical question of the profitability of business investment. The average profit margin made by British companies at home is four per cent.[87] In the Southern World generally, this margin averages 14 per cent, but in South Africa it stands at the gargantuan rate of 20-25 per cent.[88] Yet for African peoples who create this enormous wealth and comprise 85 per cent of the South African population, they appropriate a meagre 15 per cent of the national income.[89] Unlike any other country in Africa, or indeed the whole of the African World, South Africa currently represents that dialectical coalescence and crystallisation of the definitive epochal junctures that characterise the 'relationship' between the West and Africa in the past 500 years - from the slave plantations of the 'bantustans', to the monopoly capitalism of the transnational mineralogical/banking corporations of the Johannesburg-Cape Town-Pretoria conurbation.

Baronial Fiefdoms - II

It has been useful to allocate some extended space to our discussion of the intrinsic nature of British colonialism in Africa during these early phases of the historical period. Unlike other leading European colonial powers at the time, the full breadth of British atrocities in Africa as it consolidated its colonial victories on the continent, has not really been a subject that has been systematically and consistently taught, discussed, reviewed/publicised, thanks to the continuing and pervasive influence of the British 'Colonial School of African History' in 'mainstream' academia and 'popular' consciousness. As far as this School is concerned, the British conquest 'brought peace, fairness, justice and civilizations to peoples who would otherwise know only strife, tyranny, [and] injustice.'[90] And such was the influence of this School in the United States, for instance, that until recently, as the critical African American historian James Spady recalled in an excellent article on the scholarship of Chiekh Anta Diop,[91] that 'the Fages, Olivers, McCalls and others were considered the foremost authorities on African history. Even among Black scholars and publicists in the United States. Basil Davidson was widely read, discussed and taught to the exclusion of African Africanists.'

Spady's reference to Basil Davidson's scholarship here is significant because the latter is the most distinct voice of the 'liberal' wing of this School, and has thus tried to place some emphasis on Africa's civilisations prior to the (European) conquest, unlike the 'conservatives' who would either ignore or even totally reject this in their work. It is this feature of Davidson's writings on Africa that would presumably account for its 'popularity' (among African Americans?) in the curriculum of the time. Yet, not in the main dissimilar to the 'conservatives', Davidson's scholarship treats British colonial atrocities in Africa with an uncanny track of evasiveness, politeness and, at best, understatement, even as he more characteristically explores and exposes the atrocities perpetrated by other Europeans in the continent, such as the French, Portuguese or Germans. In *Africa in History*, one of Davidson's most often quoted books, he employs the space of several pages of text documenting very graphically the brutalities meted on conquered Africans by Belgian, German, Portuguese and French colonial regimes, but covers the British examples with carefully crafted sanitated phraseologies that essentially border on meaninglessness. Some examples from this publication are necessary to illustrate the point. Despite clear-cut British atrocities in Kenya, as we highlighted earlier, the following is Davidson's quaint review of this horrific occupation of east Africa:'[T]he process of imperial enclosure was more often coercive than not, and that in few cases it was violently destructive. These things may be disagreeable to remember. Yet no history can quite pass them by without a word, for the violence and destruction were also an influential part of the scene: their consequences, in effect, are with us to this day. They should not be allowed to obscure the humanitarian and civilising efforts of many excellent men and women, nor sully the reputation of many colonial officials and soldiers whose principal sins were no worse than Victorian smugness, ignorance, and insensitivity to the claims of pre-industrial peoples. Nor should they, perhaps above all, form any sort of reason for modern Africans to "blame their condition" only on the failings or excesses of colonialism.'[92] At no place in this review does Davidson empirically detail the systematic expulsions of Africans, and their incarcerations into concentration camps euphemistically termed 'reserves' by the occupation, nor does he focus acutely on the British seizure of African lands to make way for European settlements and appropriations. On the contrary, Davidson in fact exonerates these perpetrators of heinous crimes against the African humanity on the grounds of 'Victorian smugness, ignorance, and insensitivity...' Just what amounts to the 'humanitarian and civilising efforts' of the British conquest on the lives of the surviving Kikuyu, Luo, Maasai, Kipsigi, Nandi and other nations and nationalities in the region jettisoned to concentration camps? What really are the 'failings or excesses' of the British conquest? Finally, what is the agreeable or acceptable threshold to which 'modern Africans' should blame British/European atrocities of conquest on their contemporary 'condition'?

In his treatment of southern Africa, that region of extensive British strategic experimentation on racial separateness and hierarchisation, Basil Davidson could not have been more amazingly bland: 'Forced labour practices might be less frequent here, but the end-result was to prove even worse than for the Africans of the French and other equatorial lands in the Congo Basin and its periphery. As the imperial structures took shape, Africans found themselves increasingly deprived of their best land, and often enough of all their land.'[93] Elsewhere, still on the subject of southern Africa, Davidson laces this blandness with courteous sensitivity whilst responding to the outrageous defence of British imperialism as some '... moral [order] even more than material,' which was made by Alfred Milner, a one-time British chief representative in South Africa (and activist proponent of evolving apartheid during the early years of this century), when he notes:'Yet a disrespectful eye would have noticed that it was all one in the end.'[94] In contrast, Davidson approaches the atrocities committed by other European imperialists in Africa with forthright vigour. He reminds us in *Africa in History* that 14,000 Africans, if not 20,000 (quoting the French historian Catherine Coquery-Vidrovitch), died during the construction of the Congo-Ocean railway in French central Africa between 1921 and 1932.[95] As for Germany, also in the same text, Davidson takes us through a comprehensive narrative of that country's expropriation of lands and the displacement of African owners in Cameroon and Tanganyika, as well as providing statistical details of the German pogroms carried out on the Herero and Nama peoples of South West Africa (contemporary Namibia).[96] What emerges finally in this Davidson 2-track approach to European atrocities in occupied Africa - a tame, flaccid one for Britain, and a critical, rigorous one for the rest -, smacks of a selective, *and* convenient reading and presentation of history. And it should not be forgotten that Davidson's is the 'liberal'; not the 'conservative' orientation in the British 'Colonial School of African History'!

Peter Fryer, a British historian who works independently of this School, has in his book *Black People in the Empire*, provided a very informative insight into the historical and sociological circumstances in Britain at the height of the country's colonial conquests overseas which ensured that its academies, and other institutions and avenues of national cultural expression and creativity, provided a robust intellectual support for the colonial venture, and this in turn was progressively defused to the rest of the population:[97] 'Public enthusiasm for the British Empire was whipped up by the churches; by the schools (free compulsory education was introduced in 1870); by the comics and adventure stories produced for children and young people(a tremendous expansion in the publication of juvenile literature occurred in the 1870s and 1880s); by the new cheap and sensationalist press (the first halfpenny London daily was launched in 1896); by the music halls, popular plays, musical comedies and popular songs. These were the main transmission belts for the mythology of imperial glory and heroism and of racial superiority.' The enormous wealth derived from empire was of course of utmost importance to both state and people. For the state, these resources would be deployed in society to create new jobs and life improvement opportunities for the general population, so as to radically ease the ever deteriorating acute social contradictions resulting from the gruelling poverty of millions and millions within the country particularly from the working classes, itself one of the pressing motives for the colonial conquest.[98] It should never be forgotten that for the overwhelming majority of Britons, life was a dreary, claustral and poverty-stricken existence prior to the British colonial conquests overseas. Until the beginning of the 18th century, an 'idler' in the country, quite often a reference to an unemployed person in official parlance, had the letter 'R' (which stood for a 'Rogue') branded on their left shoulder.[99] During Queen Bess's reign, 'rogues were trussed up apace, and in one year commonly... three or four hundred were... devoured and eaten up by the gallows.'[100] If caught walking the highway, the 'idler' was branded with the letter 'V', which stood for 'Vagrant', 'and returned to his native city, whose slave he became, doing municipal work without pay, held in irons. If the latter tried prematurely to take their freedom, they automatically became the slaves of their employers, who whipped and chained them. They had the right to weld on the neck, arm, or leg of the slave an iron ring, as a distinctive mark to keep him from escaping. Slaves of towns or parishes subsisted into the nineteenth century, under the name of roundsmen.'[101] Earlier on during the reign of Henry VIII, a total of 72,000 'vagrants' were executed in Britain under the grotesque state law which condemned a 'vagrant' arrested for a third time 'to be executed as a hardened criminal and enemy of the common weal.'[102]

Consequently, the spoils of empire provided people in Britain, especially the wretched of the unemployed and those millions perpetually bonded to a callous aristocracy and proto-bourgeoisie with a phenomenal and unprecedented advancement in their standard of living, *including* the option of emigrating to any of the innumerable selection of countries and principalities across the world - from the western hemisphere, through most of Africa and Asia, and to Australasia - that made up this vast inheritance of conquest. Nostalgia for the 're-creation' of the historical conditions that gave rise to this inheritance continues to be a feature of both intellectual and 'popular' debates in Britain, particularly at this time in the 1990s when the state of the country's economy is in a very serious crisis with at least three million people out of work; widespread and continuing business failures, falling investments, especially in maintaining/upgrading ageing or decaying public utilities across the country; the devaluation of the pound as the country can no longer compete effectively with its trading partners in Europe and elsewhere; high levels of dispossession of home owners of their property as a result of them not maintaining regular payment on their mortgages to building societies, banks and other creditors; escalating homelessness especially in the urban areas, and an all time increase in the incidence of violent crimes. A recent article by a columnist of the London *Evening Standard* which was dedicated to the life of Cecil Rhodes, one of the most notorious barons of British imperialism in Africa, appears to sum up this continuing craving for the spoils of empire in contemporary Britain: 'For ourselves, we must dream of a future British generation which - like Rhodes's - will venture out into the world again unburdened by unwarranted guilt about our imperial past.'[103] And as if to demonstrate further the urgency to instil in the British national psyche the need to exorcise any 'unwarranted guilt' that may be lurking somewhere about the country's heinous crimes of conquest of yesteryears, the same columnist reminded his compatriots a few weeks later that British military aggression in the past was often inextricably linked to attempts to solve British *internal* social problems: 'When we were depressed as children, our parents devised means of taking our minds off our problems. A toy, an outing, a change in the routine. This is what the Government has to do now - find some bread and circuses wheeze to take our minds off this awful self-induced depression. What might it be? Long ago, declaring war on foreigners did the trick. Sending a million yobbos in uniform to some dark corner of the earth to [fight] and, while doing so, helping ourselves to any available booty there, still has a certain appeal.'[104]

So, African peoples, in the wake of the pan-European conquest of their homeland, did not have to live in an occupied Congo of Belgian King Leopold II to experience the crushing dehumanisation of Stengers's aptly painted imagery, the 'veritable hells-on-earth'. On the contrary, every occupied state in Africa, irrespective of the nationality of the occupier - Belgian, British, French, German, Italian, Portuguese, or Spanish -, was a slice of this 'veritable hells-on-earth,' where the very essence of the human rights of Africans was grotesquely violated by the imperial regime either through carefully thought-out policies, or just routinely as a feature dictated by the circumstances of the occupation. What in fact Europe does in Africa as it consolidates its occupation in the early decades of this century is to adapt, or re-enact on the local scene, the prototypes of the limitless strands of the degradation of the African humanity that it operated on a grand scale during the course of the previous 350 years, when millions of Africans laboured as slaves in the mines and plantations of the Americas and the Caribbean. Consequently, Europe's appropriation of the labour and natural resources of the African humanity universally, at home and in the diaspora, was complete. Europe had now opened up a new chapter in its perpetration of the most systematically executed assault on the human rights of a people ever known in history. Eighty years on, that is, in the world of the 1980s, Europe, and the United States of America, that colossus of the European conquest-state west of the Atlantic, would shamelessly lead a campaign to lecture the world at large on what it called 'defence of human rights within and among nations'. The irony of that cynical gimmick was of course not lost on the sensibilities of any critical observer who was conversant with the principal current of the history that we have just been reviewing, or indeed the entire trajectory of the political and economic policy of the countries of the European World to Africa, and other states in the South since 1945, namely the era of the restoration of independence following the European conquest.

Road to Restoration of Independence

As we indicated earlier, there were nine very important spheres of social existence in which Africa pursued its resistance to the European conquest. With the armed struggle component of this virtually over in most places by the end of the second decade of this century as Europe consolidated its victory, the Africans began to optimise their operations in the other eight options available to them, including those at the very heart of a maturing post-conquest economy that Catherine Coquery-Vidrovitch has pointedly described as an 'archaic economy, that is an economy that depended on taxation and plundering instead of production and investment.'[105] African workers in factories, plantations, mines and public works seized on the strike weapon as firstly a means to try to safeguard their basic interests as human beings in the atrocious working conditions that we have variously referred to in this text, and secondly as an opportunity, through their levers of organisation, to embark on laying the foundation of an alternative, proto-nationalist power base which would either spearhead the movement towards the restoration of independence later as was indeed the case in a number of countries, or link up with other constituencies of nationalist activism such as political parties (where available, or when ultimately formed), churches, schools and cultural unions for the pursuit of the same goal. The grave socio-economic deprivations and dislocations to which Africans were generally subjected during the course of the First World War (1914-1918), including the loss of 250,000 conscripts in the conflict, the impact of the partial and essentially racist settlement of the 'Colonial Question' in the 1919 Versailles treaty which ended the war (Freed all European peoples in central and eastern Europe under the vestiges of Ottoman, German, Austria-Hungarian, and, to some extent, Czarist colonialisms, whilst silent on similarly colonised peoples in Africa, and elsewhere in the Southern World. Instead, Europe reinforced its occupation of Africa; Africans in defeated German colonies were contemptuously re-colonised by Britain and France, or, as in South West Africa, placed under the political tutelage of the European-minority ruled South Africa.), and the depression of the late 1920s in the Western economy, fuelled the militancy of African workers during the period. In addition, recently demobilised soldiers from the war who now went to work on the railways, dockyards and other public services in their countries had begun to inject a certain amount of nationalist radicalism in the main discourse of trade union organisations, a point to be stressed in any serious assessment of the marked transformation of the political character and direction of strike actions across the continent subsequently. Between 1919 and 1926, for instance, there were a series of strikes in the railway networks in Sierra Leone and Nigeria,[106] strategically vital outlets for the 'cash crop' export trade of the two countries. Also in 1919, dockworkers in Conakry (Guinea) went on strike, and this was the same year that the first of two crippling general strikes in as many years was organised in the Gold Coast.[107]

Away from western to southern Africa, it is instructive to note that it was in 1919 that the militant African trade union body, the Industrial and Commercial Workers Union (ICU) was formed in South Africa to galvanise African resistance in the work place, particularly in the mines and farm settlements. This was a development that 'spread like wild fire' across the country,[108] energetically expanding the political activity of the African National Congress which had been formed seven years earlier. The ICU organised several strikes in the mine industry soon after, and such was its popularity among the African labour force that its membership shot up to 100,000 by 1926-27.[109] Predictably, the state, and other influential sectors of power and opinion in the European occupation community such as farmers who in the mean time had carried out mass dismissals of African employees belonging to the ICU in addition to the seizure of their stock,[110] reacted aggressively to the ICU strike campaigns which it planned to halt as well as destroy the trade union body all together. These tasks were achieved largely by 1932, but not without the ICU sowing the seeds of conscientising African workers throughout the country for even more sustained struggles in the future. Indeed during the course of the Second World War (1939-1945), there were over 300 strikes organised by a variegated grouping of African labour organisations in South Africa that involved at least 58,000 (African) workers.[111] In 1946, a major strike in the mine industry involving 76,000 Africans[112] underlined most dramatically the resiliency of African resistance which had been waxed so forthrightly in the activism of the ICU during the previous two decades.

Still on the colonial economy, there was another important site of African resistance initiative particularly from the 1920s which at first glance might appear contradictory. This was the growing *voluntary* involvement of African farmers and budding entrepreneurs in the 'cash crop' economy, the very basis of the European plunder of African resources and the exteriorisation of the logic of any meaningful form of production and exchange on the continent. The African initiative was to create, and possibly compete for space with the already established European merchant/farming organisations on the lucrative territory of the ever-expanding 'cash crop' trade which, for better or for worse, they reckoned would remain a very important plank in the post-conquest economy. In west Africa, for instance, small-scale farmers, relying principally on 'traditional' farming implements such as hoes and axes succeeded in providing the colonial economy with its annual requirements of key 'cash crops' such as oil palm products, cotton and cocoa, not to mention growing sufficient food for the needs of the local population.[113] This is a development that underlines most cogently Walter Rodney's critical observation of Europe's minimal 'transfer' of Western technology to occupied Africa: 'The most convincing evidence as to the superficiality of the talk about colonialism having "modernised" Africa is the fact that the vast majority of Africans went into colonialism with a hoe and came out with a hoe.'[114]

An elaboration on the importance of the private African farming initiative on the famed cocoa industry in the then Gold Coast is appropriate. With the imperial demand for the cocoa crop for its manufacturing industry back home in Europe firmly established, actual Cocoa cultivation in the Gold Coast started largely as an African local venture, concentrating on family/community farming lands in the 1890s.[115] Within ten years, the total cocoa production area in the country was 17,000 hectares, and in another twenty years, this increased to 364,000 hectares;[116] by 1934, as it still depended on this small-scale African cultivation, the Gold Coast produced 40 per cent of the world's cocoa output, and it is significant to note that the industry had 'benefitted little from [the colonial regime's] scientific research' carried out in the country.[117] In the event, these west African successes became a major contributing factor in ensuring that the occupying regimes did not resort to the establishment of extensive 'cash crop' plantation farming seen elsewhere in Africa (especially in the east, central and the south), which in turn resulted to an insignificant number of Africans in the region losing their lands.[118] Yet, even in the 'settler'-choked states of east, central/southern Africa, comparable African initiatives towards establishing some control on their economic life was evident. Until the eve of the First World War in 1914, the African 'cash crop' output in Kenya was higher than those grown by the 'settlers', and African food crop cultivators in the country, as well as in the then Southern Rhodesia, adequately rivalled the capacity of the European occupation farmers , despite the latter's well-known privileges and advantages, to provide grain for the population.[119] In former Northern Rhodesia, the occupation regime had to enact a series of laws as from the late 1920s which expropriated more lands from Africans, as a frantic measure to stem the successes of independent private African cultivation which accounted for 50 per cent of all cattle sold in the country in 1930 and 49 per cent of maize sales in 1935.[120] Africans expelled from their lands were of course interned in the new 'reserves', from where they were expected to offer themselves instead as cheap labour to the European-run farms. Defending these measures, an occupation spokesperson could not have been more honest: 'the British Empire is *primarily* concerned with the furtherance of the interests of British subjects of British race *and only thereafter* with other British subjects, protected races, and the nationals of other countries, in that order.'[121] (added emphasis)

We shall be returning to the subject of independent African initiatives later on in this book when we focus on its strategic role in the construction of a totally new civilisation of political and economic relations to overcome the grave crisis that the African humanity is currently going through. In the interim, we should emphasise that even in its apparent contradictoriness, the local independent crop producing initiative that we have been discussing were essentially socio-economic autonomising projects which had already had illustrious precedents in Africa, typified perhaps most spectacularly by the patriotism and the entrepreneurial genius of King Jaja of Opobo who in the 1880s effectively controlled the palm oil produce trade of the eastern Niger Delta and its hinterland, thereby denying, for quite a while, an expansionist British imperialism's objective of taking over this trade, the people and their lands.[122] More importantly though, these initiatives had distinct compensatory implications on the politics of the restoration of independence, especially after the end of the Second World War in 1945 when a number of the more successful farmers and businesspersons from the 'cash crop' enterprise either provided vitally needed funds required to found or sustain political parties/trade union movements/other nationalist organisations or, using the considerable influence they had built over the years in the community, led or played important roles in the independence struggle.

The World Wars and the Restoration of Independence

The course and outcome of the Second World War gave considerable impetus to Africa's struggle to free itself from the European conquest. In 1939, Britain and France declared war on Germany following the latter's invasion of Poland. Just as in the First World War two decades earlier, African conscripts soon found themselves fighting in another European-globalised war which was not of their own making. Apart from Liberia, which was at best nominally independent, and Ethiopia, the rest of Africa was under the colonial subjugation of *these same* European countries at war, except, ironically, Germany. Germany had lost its occupied African states of South West Africa (Namibia), Tanganyika (part of contemporary Tanzania), Togoland and Cameroon in 1918 as a result of its defeat in the First World War by Britain and its allies. Instead of restoring immediate independence to the peoples in these African states at the Versailles conference terminating the war, Britain, and France (incidently a very weak state in the eventual victorious alliance - barely contained Germany's invasion of its homeland only due to robust allies' intervention in the fighting; it would capitulate completely to Germany during the Second World War 25 years later), quickly incorporated the latter into their *own* existing empires (Tanganyika became British; Togoland was taken over by France, and Cameroon was split into two parts, with the north French and the south British), whilst South West Africa was 'assigned' to the European-minority ruled South Africa to 'administer', a euphemism that hardly disguised the territory's real status as Pretoria's newly acquired colony. In contradistinction, the defeat of Turkey and Austria-Hungary, Germany's central European allies in the war, resulted in the liberation of several subject peoples which included the Greeks, Poles, Slovaks, Serbs, Croats, Czechs and Rumanians. So, for Africa which lost 250,000 soldiers fighting for the conflictive territorial claims of rival European imperialist states in the 1914-18 war, the outcome of the conflict was grim indeed: continuing colonial occupation. The victorious European countries continued to maintain a contemptuous disregard for the human and national rights of the African peoples even though these states had claimed that they went to war in 1914 to confront Germany's territorial ambitions in Europe and elsewhere. As African conscripts went to fight for these same imperialist states in 1939, it was even less likely that their own independence would be secured in the event of victory against Germany.

One million African conscripts were drafted to fight for the anti-German coalition forces during World War II. All accounts record the valiant performances of the African contingents in the principal theatres of the war: western Europe; the gruesome Far East campaigns against Japan where African casualties ran into tens of thousands; north Africa/Middle East, and the preparations leading to the coalition's landings in western Europe in 1944 (the role of the African Guyanese governor of Chad, Felix Eboue, in providing logistics in west/central Africa, and in his unequivocal support for the 'Free French Forces' were crucial in the coalition's successes at this theatre), and the battles in north-east Africa in 1940/41 which led to the liberation of Ethiopia from the occupation of the Italians. Besides providing troops, African countries, particularly those in the western part of the continent free from any combat activities, also provided the anti-German allies with rear bases and supply lines especially for the north African and west European campaigns. This accounted for the massive expansion of air and sea port facilities in the west African region in 1940-43. Furthermore, the absence of fighting in the region ensured that Britain, which was now the only effective European imperialist power in Africa, with the recent fall of France to the Germans, could offset the sharp drop that occurred in the early 1940s in the global production of palm oil, groundnut, tin and rubber due to the Japanese overrun of south-east Asia. It readily stepped up the production of these commodities in occupied Nigeria, Gold Coast, Sierra Leone and the Gambia.

Germany surrendered in May 1945, and with the opposing coalition forces' victory assured, the European powers were faced with the choice of implementing the Anglo-American Atlantic Charter which was formulated in 1941. A clause in the Charter affirmed the 'right of all peoples to choose the form of government under which they will live [and] to see [the] sovereign rights and self government restored to those who have been forcibly deprived of them.'[123] But *in practice*, these powers felt that this clause did not apply to Africans (and other peoples in Asia, the Pacific, South America and the Caribbean under European colonial conquests). For Britain, its war-time prime minister and indeed a co-signatory to the Atlantic Charter, Winston Churchill, had declared categorically that he 'had not become the King's First Minister in order to preside over the liquidation of the British empire.'[124] The French, their early capitulation to Germany during the war notwithstanding, were similarly supercilious of the liberation of African, Asian and other Southern peoples from European imperialism. During the 1944 Brazzaville conference of French 'overseas' governors which was chaired by General de Gaulle, leader of the anti-German 'Free French Forces', the French position on the subject was re-stated emphatically: 'Self-government must be rejected - even in the more distant future.'[125] It should not be forgotten that as the political leaders of these so-called Free French Forces proclaimed to the world with impunity that they would continue to occupy and subjugate millions of peoples across the Southern World, they, *themselves*, constituted the movement that was spearheading the liberation of France that was, in 1944, still under the jackboot of German occupation. Belgium, the conqueror of the Congo, which barely resisted Germany's own attack on its territory beyond 18 days in June 1940, was itself equally unwilling to discontinue its occupation of this central African country after Germany's eventual defeat in 1945. This is in spite of the *central* role that the Congo played in the financing of the Belgian war effort, a point surprisingly acknowledged officially by the Belgian government-in-exile secretary for the colonies during the period:[126]

> During the war, the Congo was able to finance all the expenditure of the Belgian government in London, including the diplomatic service as well as the cost of our armed forces in Europe and Africa, a total of some £40 million. In fact, thanks to the resources of the Congo, the Belgian government in London had not to borrow a shilling or a dollar, and the Belgian gold reserve could be left intact.

It was clear, once again, that despite a major global war which was caused by Europe, and which exposed so glaringly the fundamental contradictions inherent in a world that had for most of the previous 400 years been subjugated politically, economically, militarily and culturally by its recently warring states, the political leaderships in London, Paris, Brussels and the other imperialist capitals of the continent were not prepared to pull out of Africa. The invaluable contributions that Africans made to the defeat of Germany were about to be ignored. But the historic irony was not lost on the rest of the world: Britain, France and Belgium fought against Hitlerite German racism and territorial expansionism for six gruelling years, but emerged from this war apparently oblivious to the fact that *their own form* of racism was a crucial feature of the colonial ideology that had been used to legitimise the occupation of Africa, and the rest of the Southern World for centuries. That these imperialist states were not willing to withdraw voluntarily from occupied Africa, in spite of the cataclysm of World War II, was highly indicative of the serious limitations that were evident in their publicly-declared war-time political aspirations, propaganda, and objectives, especially those directed at the human and national rights of the peoples of the world. In east Africa, for instance, British propagandists characterised the war as *'vita vya uhuru'* - *'war for freedom'*.[127] How the British must have thought that this clarion call for human emancipation would not, in turn, subvert their own occupation of that part of Africa, in addition to lands elsewhere, just baffles one's imagination!

Liberation

Africans did not of course wait for Europe to embark on a voluntary evacuation from their conquered lands after the end of the Second World War. The nationalist political parties, most of which were formed during the course, or soon after the end of the war in 1945, were now effectively national liberation movements, whose pressing task was to free their countries of the European occupation once and for all. These movements were strategically broadly based, as one would expect, considering the sociological mix of peoples that had become a very important feature of life in any of these colonies during the occupation. They therefore incorporated into their organisation the multifaceted constituencies of opinion as reflected chiefly on subjects such as nationality, religion, region, and even race, an issue which indeed was of some relevance in a few cases in east/central/ southern Africa. Yet, another form of incorporation, if not 'amalgamation', was sought by these movements. They 'appropriated', most readily, the spiritual, philosophical and, where necessary, the organisational legacies of the long stretch of resistance (in all its varying forms) that had occurred against the European occupation in their societies since, including particularly those that broke out after the end of the First World War which were no doubt a precursor to the heightened liberatory dynamism of the immediate post-World War II epoch. Apart from the obvious political legitimacy that would be achieved by 'appropriating' the legacies of the 'battles fought by forefathers and foremothers', the movements' recourse to tap into the past heritage of their people's resistance was no doubt an affirmation of the *continuing*, and therefore historical *link* that existed between the struggles of that epoch, and those that were waged before their times.[128]

There was, yet, another legacy open to the African liberation movements at this time to 'appropriate'. This was the *favourable* conjunctural imperative of the 'new world order' that was emerging as a historic perspective of the aftermath of the Second World War as from the second half of the 1940s. Whilst Britain and France, the colonial dinosaur of states that still occupied most of Africa, were part of the anti-German alliance of forces that won the war in 1945, it was nonetheless clear to the world at large that for both countries, their participation in the celebrations marking the great victory of the day was *only* possible thanks to the crucial role played in the war by the following peoples and states: (a) the sacrifice of thousands of lives of conscripts of African peoples from both occupied Africa and the Caribbean; (b) the sacrifice of thousands of Asian lives from occupied India, Indo-China and elsewhere, and (c) the United States's intervention on behalf of the coalition, and the sacrifice and heroism of the Soviet Union which bore the brunt of the alliance's war effort in the central/east European theatre where it suffered a total casualty figure of 20 million killed, or just less than one-half of the final death toll in the six-year old conflict. Essentially, contrary to the thinking of the political leaderships of these states, especially on the 'Colonial Question', Britain and France had emerged from the war as very weakened states and the liberation movement in Africa, and elsewhere, knew this, and would seize the historic opportunity to their advantage. It is therefore pertinent to note that unlike in 1919, just after the end of the First World War, when the representatives of the parties of the pan-African liberation congress met in Paris and (merely) called on European leaders gathered at the Versailles conference 'to aboli[sh]... slave and forced labor, and [implement] other reforms in [the] harsh colonial rule,' the 1945 meeting of the same congress, this time in Manchester, proclaimed to the world confidently and emphatically: '[we demand] an end to all forms of economic and political imperialism and [advocate] the use of force to attain independence for Africa, if all other methods failed.'[129]

The reference to use force, if necessary, to effect liberation was 'no idle threat,' as Harry Magdoff reminds us in his informed review of the Manchester congress, because '[these] Africa[n]... political parties were [now]... better organised, more radical, and more militant than in the past. In addition, they could now call on... African soldiers with field experience and knowledge of complex weapons gained in World War II.'[130] Furthermore, the African liberation movements would have come to the conclusion that whilst the United States's post-war declarations of support for the decolonisation of the European empires were often ambiguous and contradictory as it, *itself*, wished to inaugurate a new global hegemonic 'order' under its leadership (see following chapter for an elaboration), it was in Washington's strategic interest, at least in the short term frame, not to be opposed to the African struggle because to do so was to help to prop up the retention, by Europe, of virtually the entire territory of the most important continent of the (European) colonial world.

If the US position on the 'Colonial Question' was strewn with all sorts of contradictions, the picture was much clearer on the attitude of the other emerging 'superpower', the Soviet Union. It generally supported liberation from colonial rule in the South, and in fact declared its intention to support the process militarily. For Africa, this represented a potential ally for the future. But it was the experience, the fortunes and indeed the globalised implications of the (ultimate) successes later on in the 1940s, and through to the early 1950s, of the struggles of the national liberation movements elsewhere, in Asia (the origins of some of these movements, we should point out, were part of the anti-Japanese resistance during the course of the Second World War), that had the most profound impact on the tactics and the nature of the outcome of the African liberation. The liberation of the Indian sub-continent from Britain in 1947 was followed seven years later by the crushing defeat of the French colonial army in Vietnam, and the termination of French imperialism in the entire Indo-China. With Asia having effectively 'gone', the pressure on the African liberation movement could not have been greater! Prior to that French débâcle, was of course the victory of the Chinese Revolution in 1949. Whilst not within the mould of the general anti-'classical' colonial struggle of the age, because China was not formally under the blanket occupation of any colonial power, the leaders of the revolution had no illusions whatsoever about the 'semi-colonial' status that Western, and Japanese imperialism had reduced their country.[131] To that effect, the Chinese Revolution *was* part and parcel of the heritage of Southern World national liberating confrontations of the post-

World Wars' epoch and the lessons of its aftermath were compelling examples for Africa and the rest of the South, and, surprisingly, for Europe and the rest of the Western World even if for different reasons. For the latter, the crucial attributes of the Chinese Revolution's reconstruction programme, in the wake of victory, especially its programme of *autocentric* development, amounted to a dramatic rupture with a 'world economy' that had for 400 years served Western interests, and the 'spread' or 'repeats' of the Chinese 'example' elsewhere in the South must be stopped! Now 'forewarned' by these historic events in Asia, and with another decade to go before the freeing of Africa would begin to materialise, it is therefore not surprising that Europe had a greater success in imposing the 'developmentalism' of neocolonialism on most African economies than was the case in Asia. Coming on the eve of the African liberation in the 1960s, this was in effect part of Europe's 'rearguard' manoeuvre to pre-empt the emergence of unfettered independent states in Africa, the consequences of which we shall be focusing on soon. Be it as it may, the course of history could never have been more 'on the side' of African peoples after the Second World War to free themselves once and for all from the age long ruinous occupation of their homelands by Europe. The proclamation of Ghana's independence in 1957 by Kwame Nkrumah, the star at the 1945 Manchester deliberations of the pan-African congress, set off a seismic wave of liberatory activity that would within thirty years radically transform the struggles of African peoples in Africa and elsewhere - especially in Europe, the Caribbean and the Americas, particularly the United States.

Notes

1. Chinweizu, *Decolonising the African Mind* (Lagos: Pero,1987), pp.109-135.

2. On these African civilisations, see Cheikh Anta Diop, *The African Origin of Civilization: Myth or Reality* (Westport: Lawrence Hill Books, 1974) and G. Mokhtar (ed.), *General History of Africa, Vol. II: Ancient Civilizations of Africa* (Paris/London: Unesco and Heinemann Educational Books, 1985).

3. Cheikh Anta Diop, *Precolonial Black Africa: A Comparative Study of the Political and Social System of Europe and Black Africa, from Antiquity to the Formation of Modern States*. Westport: Lawrence Hill Books, 1987), P.172.

4. Ibid., pp.172-173.

5. Ibid., pp.171-172.

6. See, for instance, Ali Mazrui, *Cultural Forces in World History* (London:James Currey, 1990).

7. See D.T.Niane, in Niane, (ed.), *Unesco General History of Africa: Vol. IV - Africa from the Twelfth to sixteenth century* (Paris/London:Unesco and Heinemann Education Books, 1984), *passim*.

8. See, for instance, *Precolonial Black Africa*, op.cit., especially ch. 7.

9. Chinweizu, op.cit., p.134.

10. Basil Davidson, *Africa in History* (London: Paladin Books, 1978) p.73.

11. Diop, op.cit., p.67.

12. Mokwugo Okoye, *Embattled Men: Profiles in Social Adjustment* (Enugu: Fourth Dimension, 1980), p.59.

13. See Ifi Amadiume, 'Gender, Political Systems and Social Movements in Africa - A West African Experience' (Paper for Codesria Project on Social Movements, Social Transformation and the Struggle for Democracy in Africa, Dakar, 1990); Amadiume, 'Writing an African Social History and Sociology of History' (Paper for Codesria Workshop on Anthropology in Africa: Past, Present and Emerging Visions, Dakar, 1991); Amadiume, *Afrikan Matriarchal Foundations: The Igbo Case* (London: Karnak House, 1987), and Amadiume, *Male Daughters, Female Husbands: Gender and Sex in an African Society* (London: Zed Books, 1987).

14. Amadiume, Male Daughters, Female Husbands, op.cit., and *passim*.

15. Amadiume, 'Gender, Political Systems and Social Movements in Africa...' op.cit., p.11.

16. Ibid., p.2.

17. Ibid., p.3.

18. Chinweizu, op.cit., p.129.

19. Quoted in Diop, op.cit., p.136.

20. Chinweizu, op.cit., p.129.

22. Williams, *The Destruction of the Black Civilisation* (Chicago: Third World, 1987), p.158.

23. Hill, 'Lies about crimes,' *The Guardian* (London), 29 May 1989.

24. Quoted in Ibid.

25. Ibid.

26. Ibid; Walter Rodney, *How Europe Underdeveloped Africa* (London: Bogle-L'ouverture, 1972), especially ch.3 and 4, and *passim*; Eric Williams, *Capitalism and Slavery* (London: Andre Deutsch, 1964); Chinweizu, *The West and the Rest of Us* (New York: Random House, 1975).

27. Michel Beaud, *A History of Capitalism: 1500-1980* (New York: Monthly Review, 1983), p.44.

28. Diop, op.cit., p.142

29. Ibid., p.47

30. Ibid.

31. Ibid.

32. Ibid.

33. Ibid., pp.110-111.

34. See Walter Rodney, 'The African Revolution,' in Paul Buhle, (ed.), *C.L.R. James: His life and work* (London/New York: Alison & Busby, 1986), pp.30-48; *Tarikh*, Vol.4, Nos 3 and 4, 1973 (Various authors) and A. Adu Boahen, (ed.), *Unesco General History of Africa: Vol VII - Africa Under Colonial Domination 1800-1935* (Paris/London:Unesco and Heinemann Education Books, 1985). (Various authors)

35. Quoted in Rodney, 'The African Revolution,' in Buhle, (ed.), op.cit., p.35.

36. Immanuel Wallerstein, 'The Three Stages of African Involvement in the World-Economy,' in Peter Gutkind and Immanuel Wallerstein, (eds.), *The Political Economy of Contemporary Africa* (California and London: Sage Publications 1976), p.39.

37. Ibid.

38. Claude Ake, *A Political Economy of Africa* (Harlow: Longman Group, 1981), p.54.

39. Ibid.

40. Ibid., p.53.

41. Ibid.

42. Ibid., p.53.

43. Quoted in Wallerstein, op.cit., p.40.

44. Ibid., p.41; Davidson, op.cit., p.263; Rodney, *How Europe Underdeveloped Africa*, op.cit., p.180 and J.C. Caldwell, 'The social repercussions of colonial rule: demographic aspects,' in Adu Boahen, (ed.),

op. cit., p.473.

45. For a recent excellent study of the brutish migratory labour regime in South Africa, see Laurie Flynn, *Studded with Diamonds and Paved with Gold: Miners, Mining Companies and Human Rights in Southern Africa* (London: Bloomsbury).

46. Quoted in Wallerstein, op.cit., p.42.

47. Cf. Rodney, *How Europe Underdeveloped Africa*, op.cit., p.182; Rodney, 'The Colonial Economy,' in A. Adu Boahen(ed.), op. cit., p.337 and Caldwell, op.cit., p.475.

48. See Ake, op.cit., p.68.

49. Ibid., p.69.

50. Ibid.

51. Rodney, *How Europe Undeveloped Africa*, op.cit., p.164.

52. Ibid., p.224.

53. Ibid.

54. Ibid., p.164

55. Ibid.

56. See D.C. Ohadike, 'Exploitation of Labour: Waged and Forced,' in Toyin Falola, *Britain and Nigeria: Exploitation or Development?* (London and New Jersey: Zed Books, 1987), pp.150-51, and *passim.*

57. Ibid., p.154.

58. S.N. Nwabara, *Iboland: A Century of Contact with Britain 1860-1960* (London: Hodder and Stoughton, 1977), p.219.

59. Peter Fryer, *Black People in the British Empire: An Introduction* (London: Pluto, 1989), p.55.

60. Nwabara, op.cit., p.154.

61. Ibid.

62. Ohadike, op.cit., p.156.

63. See Fryer, op.cit., p.157.

64. Ohadike, op.cit., p.156.

65. Ibid., *passim.*

66. Ibid., p.157.

67. Rodney, *How Europe Underdeveloped Africa*, op.cit., p.167.

68. Ibid., pp.167-68.

69. M.H.Y. Kaniki, 'The colonial economy: the former British zones,' in Boahen (ed.), op.cit., p.386.

70. Quoted in Rodney, *How Europe Underdeveloped Africa*, op.cit., p.180.

71. Anonymous, *Independent Kenya* (London: Zed, 1982), p.6.

72. Rodney, op.cit., pp.168-69, and *passim.*

73. Fryer, op.cit., p.35.

74. Ibid.
75. Ibid.
76. Ibid.
77. Rodney, op.cit., p.165.
78. Fryer, op. cit., p.165.
79. Quoted in Ibid., p.47.
80. Ibid., p.43.
81. Ibid.
82. Rodney, op.cit., p.166.
83. See Ann Seidmann and Neva Seidmann Makgetla, *Outposts of Monopoly Capitalism: Southern Africa in the Changing Global Economy* (Westport/ London: Lawrence Hill and Zed, 1980), pp.69-80.
84. Ibid., p.80.
85. Herbert Ekwe-Ekwe, 'South Africa: The Agony of Thatcherism,' *The Guardian* (Lagos), 27 July 1986.
86. Ibid.
87. Ibid.
88. Ibid.
89. Ibid.
90. Fryer, op.cit., p.57.
91. James G. Spady, 'The Changing Perception of C.A. Diop and his Work: The Preeminence of a Scientific Spirit,' in Ivan Van Sertima, ed., *Great African Thinkers, Vol.1: Cheikh Anta Diop* (New Brunswick & Oxford: Transaction Books, 1986), p.89.
92. Davidson, op.cit., p.270.
93. Ibid., p.268.
94. See Basil Davidson, *et al*, *Southern Africa: The New Politics of Revolution* (Harmondsworth: Penguin Books, 1976), p.24.
95. Davidson, *Africa in History*, op.cit., pp.266-67.
96. Ibid., pp.267-268; pp.270-273.
97. Fryer, op.cit., p.55.
98. Ibid., ch. 9 especially, and *passim*.
99. Diop, *Precolonial Black Africa*, op.cit., p.146.
100. Quoted in ibid.
101. Ibid.
102. Ibid., p.145.
103. Peter McKay, 'Hating Cecil, but loving his money,' *Evening Standard* (London), 11 January 1993, p.13.
104. Peter McKay, 'A nation in need of treatment,' *Evening Standard* (London), 25 February 1993, p.13.

105. C. Coquery-Vidrovitch, 'The colonial economy of the former French, Belgian and Portuguese zones, 1914-35,' in Boahen (ed.), op.cit., p.358.
106. Ake, op.cit., p.69.
107. Ibid.
108. Quoted in Dan O'Meara, *Volkskapitalisme* (Cambridge: Cambridge Univeristy Press, 1983), p.28.
109. See *Focus on Southern Africa* (London: Africa Centre, 1985), p.31.
110. Merle Lipton, *Capitalism and Apartheid* (Aldershot: Gower, 1985), p.101.
111. Focus on Southern Africa, op.cit., p.31.
112. Ibid.
113. Kaniki, op.cit., p.391 and p.393.
114. Rodney, *How Europe Underdeveloped Africa*, op.cit., p.239.
115. Kaniki, op.cit., pp.393-394.
116. Ibid., p.394.
117. Ibid.
118. Ibid., p.391.
119. Ibid., p.394.
120. Ibid., p.395.
121. Quoted in ibid.
122. See Obaro Ikime, 'Colonial Conquest and African Resistance in the Niger Delta,' *Tarikh* (Lagos), Vol.4 No.3, 1973, pp.1-13.
123. Quoted in A.N. Porter and A.A. Stockwell, *British Imperial Policy and Decolonisation, 1938-1964. Vol I: 1938-51* (Basingstoke and London: Macmillan, 1987), p.103.
124. Ibid., p.25.
125. Quoted by Hubert Deschambs, 'France in Black Africa and Madagascar between 1920 and 1945,' in L.H. Gann and Peter Duiganan, (ed.), *Colonialism in Africa, 1870-1960. Vol.Two: The History and Politics of Colonialism 1914-1960* (Cambridge University Press, 1970), p.249.
126. Quoted by Rodney, op.cit., p.188.
127. Basil Davidson, '1945 & All That,' *Marxism Today* (London), May 1985, p.17.
128. Cf. Rodney, 'The African Revolution,' op.cit., p.34, and *passim*.
129. See summary of key resolutions of both the Second Pan African Congress (Paris, 1919) and the Fifth Pan-African Congress (Manchester, 1945) in Harry Magdoff, *Imperialism: From the Colonial Age to the Present* (New York and London: Monthly Review), 1978, p.67.
130. Ibid.
131. See, for instance, Mao Tse-Tung, 'On Contradiction,' in Mao Tse-Tung, *Five Essays on Philosophy* (Peking:Foreign Language Press, 1977) pp.23-78.

Actually we had all been duped. No independence was given - it is never given but taken, anyway. Europe had only made a tactical withdrawal on the political front and while we sang our anthem and unfurled our flag she was securing her iron grip behind us in the economic field. And our leaders in whose faces we hurled our disenchantment neither saw nor heard because they were not leaders at all but marionettes... So the problem remains for Africa, for black people, for all deprived peoples and for the world...

Chinua Achebe, *Contemporary Poets*, 1980

Chapter 2

Restoration of Independence - A Song of Ourselves?

On the morrow of the restoration of African independence, the celebration of the historic occasion was cruelly tempered by the realisation of the depth of the scourge of inheritance that was the colonial conquest economy. In Ghana, in 1957, the leadership of the liberation movement under Kwame Nkrumah discovered to its astonishment that in the previous 30 years alone, ' British trading and shipping interests took out of our country a total of £300,000,000.'[1] 'Just imagine,' Nkrumah speculated, ' what might have been done by way of development if only part of these gigantic transfers of profit had been retained and used for the benefit of the people...'[2] In spite of the fact that the Gold Coast had for nearly 50 years then been the world's largest cocoa producer, 'there was not a single chocolate factory [here]. While we produce the raw materials for the manufacture of soap and edible fats, palm products, the manufacture of these items was discouraged. A British firm owning lime plantations here... actually expresses the juice from the fruit before shipping it in bulk to the United Kingdom and exporting it back to us, bottled, to retail in stores at a high price...'[3] Nkrumah's conclusion on this sordid legacy could not have been more graphically put: 'These facts have a kind of Alice in Wonderland craziness about them... They are implicit in the whole concept and policy of colonialism.'[4] In Nigeria, where the restoration of the people's independence occurred in 1960, another dimension of this legacy of European conquest is acutely illustrated by the basic health statistics of the country bequeathed by Britain. On the eve of the liberation of Nigeria, the country had one doctor to serve every 133,000 people, at a time when Britain had one to every 3,700 people back in its homeland.[5] One hospital bed was available for every 3,700 inhabitants in the country, whilst the figure in Britain was one for every 250 people. The infant mortality rate was generally twice as high as that of Britain's. Tuberculosis was rife, accounting for about 10 per cent of the total mortality in the country. Despite this, there was no sanatorium in the country. Thus, the treatment of the disease in general hospitals ensured its unchecked spread. Even though Nigeria possessed the most 'diversified' of British-occupied African economies, in the sense that it had a greater variety of 'cash crops' and minerals which it produced for the European World market, 80 per cent of its population then were still classified as 'living by very low-order subsistence agriculture.'[6] Just about 10 per cent of the estimated eight million children who were less than 16 years of age were in school.[7] In Tanzania, on the eve of the restoration of independence (1961), the country had 14 African medical doctors, and just one African lawyer,[8] whilst in neighbouring Zambia (restoration of independence: 1964), the legacy of the British conquest on the development of the country's 'skilled' humanpower capability was clearly evident by its absence: 'African education had... received little serious attention during the colonial period and there was an acute shortage of educated, skilled and trained manpower... [T]here was a paucity of indigenous control of key sectors of the economy with foreign firms and non-citizens owning and controlling most industry, commerce, financial institutions and commercial agriculture.'[9] But it was in Portuguese-occupied Africa that this scourge of inheritance of a conquest economy was most painfully evident. Four hundred years after the occupation, Portugal 'had not managed to train a single African doctor in Mozambique [restoration of independence: 1975], and life expectancy in Eastern Angola [restoration of independence: 1975] was less than 30 years. As for Guinea-Bissau [restoration of independence: 1974], some insight into the situation there is provided by the admission of the Portuguese themselves that Guinea-Bissau was more neglected than Angola and Mozambique!'[10] Finally, a glance at a similar portfolio of statistics on South Africa, that last bastion of European World rule in Africa yet to be liberated as these lines are written. These should alert any interested observer of the enormity of societal reconstruction work that the first African post-liberation leadership must face, and should be a reminder, given its contemporaneity, of the tasks which a host of African leadership had to contend with 25-30 years ago. In 1982-84, on the eve of the outset of the concerted African uprising that finally forced the apartheid state into its death throes, the following statistics[11] characterise the gravity of an inheritance that will surely be central in the liberation administration's painstaking compilation of a priority order list of action. In 1982, African infant mortality was 80 deaths in the first year per 1000 live births, whilst that of Europeans was 14 deaths. The situation was of course worse in the 'bantustans'. In Transkei, for instance, the figure was 190 deaths per 1000 live births. About 30 per cent of African children in the country who were less than 14 years of age were classified as 'underweight and stunted in growth,' with no comparable recorded statistics on this feature for the European. In the 'bantustans', the figure increases sharply, reaching two-thirds of the children within the same age bracket above in some cases. Three hundred and thirty seven Africans had access to one hospital bed, during the period, compared to 61 Europeans to one bed. At a roughly equivalent period in Nigeria, namely 20 years before the termination of British colonialism, the patient-bed access ratios for the two races here were *in fact* worse than comparable figures for South Africa. In Ibadan (western Nigeria) then, 50 Europeans who lived in the town had access to an 11-bed specially equipped hospital, while the African population of the town which numbered 500,000 just had a 34-bed ordinary hospital![12] Finally on South Africa, a note on the apartheid regime's expenditure on education during the 1983-84 financial year: for Africans, 234 rands per individual in the population was allocated, while the European figure was at least seven times as much per individual - 1,654 rands.[13]

The above snap-shots represent merely a randomly selected sample from a scorched earth file which points to the very essence of an economy that was to serve as the basis for the extensive African programme of *reconstruction*, following the termination of the European colonial conquest. It was clear that the task facing Africa in the morning after liberation was daunting indeed. It amounted literally to embarking on the reconstruction of a battered economy, in order then to *reconstruct* the entire society itself. Or was it?

As the pressures of the national liberation movements mounted across the entire Southern World after the end of World War II in 1945, it was becoming apparent that the European imperialist states, contrary to their publicly-held intransigent opposition to the process, were rethinking their entire 'colonial policy' of how to 'adjust' to an increasingly inevitable outcome: defeat. The freeing of India (1947), and the victory of the Chinese Revolution (1949) had strategically strengthened this possibility of European defeat as we indicated in the last chapter. As we also pointed out in the last chapter, the routing of the French colonial army by Vietnamese revolutionaries (1954) effectively sealed the fate of European colonialism in the South. By the mid-1950s therefore, it was clear that except where there was an 'appreciable' number of European 'settlers'(Kenya, Algeria, Guinea-Bissau, Cape Verde, Namibia, Angola, South Africa, Mozambique, Zimbabwe), Europe had now to contend seriously with the imminent liberation of its occupied Southern World. The 'exception' made on the above listed countries was historically significant, as it signalled, even if implicitly, the *decisive* shift that had occurred, just within a decade, in the balance of power between the occupation forces and the liberation movements. The fact that this shift was in the latter's advantage meant that the only 'factor' that could now delay or block the liberation of the 'settler colonies' was the 'settlers' themselves, not the European homeland as would have been the case until lately. In other words, given their *physical presence on the ground*, it was now the direct responsibility of the 'settlers' to defend the occupation if they had to stop the tide of nationalist liberation! One is not implying here that Europe, or indeed the West as a whole (as the United States began to feature more prominently in the 'management' of this 'new' post-World War II 'world order'), was going to abandon its kith and kin in these 'exceptional colonies' to an 'uncertain future', but that it could not win indefinite counter-insurgency wars in these countries. Europe of course came to the support of its cousins as the nationalist revolutionaries fought to free their countries subsequently.

It is also historically significant that all these 'exceptional colonies' were in Africa. They would all be later freed through armed struggle. In the meantime, however, the European World's frantic calculations on how to respond to the 'inevitability' of liberation in the 'non-settler colonies' of Africa, 10 years after the breakthrough in Asia, was inextricably linked to strategies it was developing and deploying to 'contain' insurgent developments in the former as seen for instance in Kenya, Guinea-Bissau and Algeria where liberation wars had already been launched by the mid-'50s. Pointedly, all the three insurgencies just mentioned began before the historic 1957 nationalist freeing of 'non-settler colony' Ghana.

As we hinted earlier on in the last chapter, the lessons of Asian liberation were not lost on Europe. With the breathing space of at least a decade, Europe was able to construct a *neocolonial* alternative to an unfettered restoration of African independence. For the European World, there was no question whatsoever of coming to terms with total African liberation. This was inconceivable. This outcome was ruled out. Africa was too strategic a proposition to 'let go'.

On this score, Europe was elated by the United States's position on the 'Colonial Question' which had now become more definitive since it was originally broached by President Roosevelt in his Second World War-time (1941) summit with British Prime Minister Churchill. Since the US establishment 'Grand Area' planners[14] who, during the course of the war, worked out parts of the world that were 'strategically necessary for [the United States] world control' (i.e., 'open to investment, the repatriation of profits, access to resources and so on - and dominated by the United

States.'[15]), the principal European occupying powers in the Southern World (Britain and France particularly) had remained unsettled about the implication of this geo-strategic conceptualisation on their relative positions in the 'new world order' that emerged in 1945. This was for two, interrelated, reasons. First, the 'Grand Area' envisaged by the Americans included the *entire* Southern World in its geographical spread[16] - in effect, incorporating all countries and peoples that made up the European empires. Secondly, the public rhetoric under which US state officials and publicists pursued the implementation of this 'new order' was the 'right of all peoples to choose the form of government under which they will live',[17] a formulation contained in the 'Atlantic Charter' and which had caused too much dissension in Britain soon after the Roosevelt-Churchill summit because it clearly expressed the rights of *all* oppressed peoples to national liberation.

Within five years of the end of the war, these European powers realised that they needn't get too perturbed about the US 'Grand Area' programme. Whilst the US was no doubt the most powerful country that had emerged in the Western World at the end of the war, it was soon clear that Washington required the cooperation of these Europeans to effectively run the 'new world order' which was becoming more 'complicated' in its evolution. After all, they represented the prime 'survivors' of the leadership of the 'old imperialist world order' whose 'experience' of 'global management' in the past was still likely to be of immense benefit to the United States. Furthermore, they had acknowledged unquestionably the US political, military and economic supremacy during the recently concluded war with Germany and its allies. The latter consideration may have contributed enormously to the US modification of the original conception of the 'Grand Area' in the way that this affected the overall character of the 'core-states' which made up the leadership of the 'new order'. Instead of embarking on the task singularly, Washington now decided to 'broaden' the leadership by assigning important roles to Britain and France to play in international relations especially in several supranational organisations which had been formed after the war such as the United Nations, the World Bank, the IMF and the International Court of Justice, not to mention the more exclusive military alliance, the North Atlantic Treaty Organisation. It should be pointed out that in constructing a pan-hegemonic concert of states where its supreme leader was accorded full 'recognition' by all the 'core states', the United States of America succeeded in instilling a vital measure of 'stability' among the West's imperialist states for the first time since the European World conquest of the world began in the 15th century. It was the absence of this 'stability', exacerbated by the 'non-recognition' of a clear-cut leader that fuelled the acute intra-imperialist rivalries of the past which ended with two major wars erupting between 1914 and 1939.

Besides the outbreak of the Cold War between the West and the Soviet-led East bloc which would become as frosty as ever in the years ahead, the most important political development of the immediate post-World War II era was of course the struggle of the national liberation movement in the South. Already, the radical nationalism of the movement in Asia (anti-French resistance in Indo-China, Chinese Revolution) had opened up a range of possibilities for the realisation of a *genuine* restoration of independence from the European World. They unambiguously advocated the total control of their society's resources (human and non-human), the democratisation of the institutions of decision-making and the transformation of the peoples' living standards. But these were precisely the sort of goals of the Southern liberation movement which ran contrary to the critical tenets of the United States's 'Grand Area' conceptualisation of the 'new world order'.[18] Britain and France, among others of the imperialist powers in the South, could not have agreed more. Quite clearly, the United States and the principal states of the European pre-World War II 'world order' found much sooner than they would have hoped for after the war that they had no fundamental disagreement over the 'containment' nor indeed the blocking of genuine national liberating initiatives in the Southern World. On the contrary, it was in their mutual interest as evident in the cooperation and/or solidarity that these powers shared in confronting radical national liberation movements in the South in the subsequent 40 years: China, Vietnam, Cambodia, Tamil Eelam, Kenya, Algeria, Guinea-Bissau, Angola, Mozambique, Eritrea, Biafra, Namibia, South Africa, Zimbabwe, Cuba, Grenada, Nicaragua, Iran, Palestine. For the United States therefore, the restoration of independence in the European-occupied Southern World after the end of the war in 1945 was at best a version of the Latin American experience where an entire continent had in spite of nearly 200 years of independence been converted into an American strategic and economic fiefdom, or what Washington prefers, more contemptuously, to describe as its 'backyard'. Watching nervously in the early 1950s as the drama of the African liberation struggle unfolded, Britain, France, Belgium, Portugal and Spain did not fail to learn from this US example.

Foundations of Neocolonialism

Apart from embarking on the construction of the political edifice locally that would maintain in perpetuity the disarticulated African economy[19] that served the West, the European powers during the period were virtually engrossed in a vulturous drive to transfer as much as African capital resources as they could manage before their imminent departure. The situation was very much comparable to the rogue who, conscious of the limited time available to complete their deed, stole and stole and stole in order to build up a convenient reserve. Africa would probably have been lucky if only the rogue was content with their reserve. No, in the classic Dickensian insatiableness, they still wanted more and more and more... The grotesque impoverishment of the African socio-economic landscape which was subsequently 'inherited' by the African liberation government attest to this furacious outrage by Europe.

Some elaboration of the extent of this outrage is necessary here. In 1945, Africa's contribution to Britain's sterling balance was £446 million.[20] By 1955, two years before the liberation of Ghana, Africa's transfers to this sterling balance increased by at least three-fold to £1,446 million. This figure represented over one-half of the total sum of British/Commonwealth gold and dollar reserves which was £2,120 million.[21] These sterling balances were in fact a 'form of forced saving' to which Britain had decreed that each of its occupied country in Africa and elsewhere must contribute.[22] 'The ... balances were generally invested in long-term British government securities. In other words, the colonies were lending money to Great Britain. Moreover, the interest rates on these securities were extremely low: 0.5 per cent before 1950; from 2 to 4 per cent after 1952'[23] These balances were not only an invaluable resource for Britain to finance the war against Germany (on the eve of the war, the balances stood at £500 million and was over £3000 million at the end of the conflict[24], but also for the painful post-war reconstruction of the late 1940s/1950s as shown in the following figures indicating the spiralling increase of the funds then:[25] 30 June 1945: £670 million; 31 December 1950: £735 million; 30 June 1951: £908 million; 30 June 1954: £1,183 million and 30 June 1956: £1,301 million.

Responding to the British reconstruction programme, its occupied Nigeria government embarked on an intensification of both the country's agricultural and mineral products - especially palm products, cotton, rubber, hides and skins, beniseeds, groundnuts, tin ore and columbite.[26] In

1946, the value of Nigerian exports was £23.7 million.[27] By 1955, it was £129.8 million, and in 1960, the year of the restoration of independence, it was £165.5 million.[28] There was a distinct growth in Nigeria's gross domestic product during the period, an annual rate of 4.1 per cent in 1950/51-1957/58.[29] Indeed, not since 1916 had Nigeria enjoyed a favourable net-barter terms of trade with Britain as was recorded between 1951-55, and 1958-60.[30] But Nigeria was still a British-occupied country, with a political economy that existed solely to serve British imperialist interests. This was underlined by the fact that the huge sum of £276.8 million, the preponderant chunk of the surpluses that accumulated from this unprecedented boom, was transferred to Britain between 1947-1960.[31] This is not to mention British surpluses enjoyed by the corresponding increases in the value of Nigerian imports from mainly Britain at the time: £19.8 million in 1946, £136.1 million in 1955, and £215.9 million in 1960.[32] Besides, Britain's more advantageous trade relations with Nigeria were further consolidated in 1955 when Europe slumped into an economic recession. The prices that Europeans were prepared to pay for imports of agricultural and mineral products from abroad fell considerably, resulting in an instant blow to the Nigerian economy. Even though its export trade that year increased by 7,000 tons in volume, the value fell by £17 million.[33]

In the 1950s, Sierra Leone, its very small economy notwithstanding, made a contribution of £60 million to the British sterling balances[34]. Gold Coast's (Ghana) total was £210 million by 1955.[35] The latter's transfer was even more significant for Britain because a high percentage of this sum (60-80 %) was in American dollars which the Gold Coast earned by selling cocoa to the United States.[36] Britain was badly in need of dollars to purchase US capital products to reconstruct its war-battered industrial enterprises. Apart from Malaya, the Gold Coast made the highest contribution to these sterling balances, including their dollar component, during the period.[37] Bob Fitch and Mary Oppenheimer have observed: 'Much [has been] made of the sacrifices made by the British [public] during the period [of post-World War II reconstruction]. Yet to a large extent it was the Asian and African peasant who played the decisive role and experienced the real "austerity".'[38] And a British-based financial commentator did not fail to detect the historical irony of these net Southern capital transfers to a Western country when he wrote in 1953: 'the investment of £1,000 million in Britain does not accord well with commonly held ideas on the desirable direction of capital flow between countries at different levels of economic development.'[39] It is interesting to note that the key phrase in the above quote is 'desirable direction of capital flow'. Whilst the observer may have been responding to an anguished prick on his *own* conscience about statistics that we must stress only focus on a minute scale of the European World's predacious escapades in Africa, and elsewhere in the South, it is not at all certain from whose point of view (European World or the African) that a 'desirable direction of capital flow' could be contemplated, and implemented! It would be of immense delight to examine how the same commentator would respond to the contemporary record of African net capital transfers to the West (see next chapter),which makes the statistics of 40 years ago appear as pennies in a piggy-bank.

Kwame Nkrumah's famous aphorism of the era, 'seek first the political kingdom', probably smacks of political naivety, if not opportunism for a conscientious student of the 1990s' African political scene. Such a latter judgement may indeed be unfair, especially given the inevitable advantages provided by hindsight. What is however certain is that the above declaration was a clear admission by one of the most articulate leaders of the African liberation movement at the time, that the struggle for the restoration of independence was fraught with immense difficulties particularly on the economic front. The tentacles of Western neocolonial structures continued to expand most menacingly either in Ghana itself, as we have just shown and where Nkrumah had become prime minister following the 1957 liberation, or elsewhere where freedom was imminent. Ghana's disastrous economic performance during the first four years of liberation pointedly occurred when the Nkrumah administration pursued its 'Open-Door Policy' which continued to enhance the dominant position of Western business interests in the country, whilst restricting the involvement of Ghanaians especially in the lucrative mining, insurance, timber contracting and the import-export trade.[40] The outcome of this programme was another bout in the country's now legendary net capital outflow to the West. Fitch and Oppenheimer estimate that the figure for this net capital transfer for the four years was £6.5 million[41] but the distinguished Ghanaian historian, Adu Boahen reckoned that it was much higher than that - £28 million.[42] If anyone wanted proof of what really constituted the West's strategic goal in Africa, these early economic results from seemingly independent Ghana were there for public perusal! In the event, these results reinforced the position of a number of pan-African intellectuals then resident in Ghana who had advised Nkrumah to proclaim the country's independence as early as 1951 so as to pre-empt, if not scuttle the maturation of the British neocolonial institutions which were already being grafted to all the critical sectors of the political economy soon after the end of the Second World War.[43] If the 'political kingdom' could ever be isolated from the 'economical', even if by a thin margin, then these early developments in Ghana must have seriously called into question whether Africa had really captured the former in the first place!

Europe was less circumspect in finding a definition for these events in Ghana and elsewhere. The United States experience with Latin America became pivotally invaluable, since it demonstrated the process in which that region was converted into a US 'back-yard'. The subsequent American 'pioneering' scholarship of what came to be known as 'modernisation studies' or 'development studies' or 'westernisation'(especially works by W.W. Rostow, Gabriel Almond, G. Bingham Powell, Sidney Verba, Lucian Pye, Leonard Binder, David Eaton, Edward Shils, James Coleman, and Samuel Huntington) became compulsory references for European scholars and researchers on Africa who until lately would have been working as 'experts' in an anthropology or some other 'exotic' academic department, but who were now getting prepared to move into new 'development studies' departments sprouting all over the place across European universities. Overnight, the key words 'developing', or 'modernising', or 'westernising' became nothing more than eurocentrically-charged ideological labels strapped onto Ghana and other African countries which were then being *conjuncturally* transformed into neocolonial economies to perpetuate even further the Western control of these societies. At least evident, albeit implicitly, in the general conceptual thrust of this 'development' theorisation was that these African countries *were yet* to be developed even after all the long years of the Western territorial occupation including 400 years in Guinea-Bissau, Angola and Mozambique. So, what was the West doing in Africa all that time?!

An important element that has underlined the predominant current of 'modernisation/development' theory since the late 1950s has been the notion of the existence of the 'dual economy' in Africa and other countries of the Southern World: the 'modern' and the 'traditional'. In this regard, 'development' economists have argued that one of the factors that accounts for the continuing 'underdevelopment' of these societies is the 'coexistence' of these sectors which they categorise as 'mutually antagonistic'. The task of national 'development', they contend, must incorporate clearly mapped-out policies which energetically extend the 'modern' sector into the 'traditional'. Perhaps the most compelling commentator on this view of 'development' is W.W. Rostow, as shown in his two often-quoted books, *Stages of Economic Growth* (Cambridge: 1960) and *The Economies of Take-off into Sustained Growth* (Cambridge: 1963).

The 'dual economy' component of 'modernisation', and its other integrative variables, soon came under greater scientific scrutiny. The most important flaw that critics were quick to note was that the concept was strikingly ahistorical. Firstly, it contained no reference to the distorted and destructive consequences of the European conquest - clearly underlining its eurocentric project. Secondly, it was false to view the 'traditional' as some pre-conquest socio-economic 'mode' or a residue from the distant past. On the contrary, the 'traditional' sector was essentially a 'reserve' which the West exploited through the intermediary of the 'modern'. Walter Rodney elaborates: 'The supposedly dynamic modern enclave and the backward traditional forms were dialectically interrelated and interdependent. Growth in the export sector was possible only because it could constantly alienate value from the African communities in the form of land, labour, agricultural tribute and capital. The stagnation within these communities was induced rather than inherent.'[44] Africa's subsequent liberation must aim at the transformation of this false dichotomisation of the 'modern' and the 'traditional', possible only with the African disengagement from the current 'international' economy as we shall argue in the next chapter.

The best empirical study carried out in Africa in recent years that underpin the theoretical premise of Rodney's insights above is the study on canoe fishing in, quite significantly, Ghana. This was carried out by the researcher, Emile Vercruijsse in the 1970s and was later published as *The Penetration of Capitalism: A West African Case Study*. Vercruijsse examined the country's important labour-intensive canoe enterprise. He observed that despite the extensive growth of the state-supported 'modern' sector fishing industry (mainly capital-intensive) since the 1950s, canoe fishing ('traditional' sector) was still accounting for 'more than 50 per cent of the marine fish landed in Ghana, and had increased its production by some 300-400 per cent.'[45] Vercruijsse also showed that the increase in productive output of canoe-fishing had been achieved by a labour force that had hardly increased; the tremendous growth was rather due to an increase in labour productivity, the replacement of a large fleet of medium-sized canoes, and the introduction of larger multi-purpose nets and outboard motors.

Following these startling results, Vercruijsse investigated the dynamics of social contradictions between the owners of the canoes and their crews. These were incipient and uneven: some canoe owners who would be classically classified as 'employers of labour' also worked as 'ordinary' members of the crews on other vessels, underlining the crucial dynamic flexibility of the use and 'movement' of labour. Even when the canoe owner went out to sea with the crew (quite often the case), the tasks on board between the former and the (rest of the) crew were interchangeable. Thus the crew members, as primary producers, were not 'proletarian producers' (they did not receive a money wage for the 'sale of their labour power') but actively participated in the sharing system which allocated the quantity of fish landed after the trip. But neither were they 'petty-commodity producers' as the sharing system involved a 'predetermined formula' weighted in favour of the canoe owner. This was why Vercruijsse categorised the crew members as an 'intermediate' social force: in a position 'somewhere in between that of the petty producer and the proletarian.'[46] The immediate consequence of this phenomenon which appeared as a restrained development of labour or what the author termed the 'incomplete nature of the dissolution of labour,'[47] was that a generalised process of 'proletarianisation' was prevented from developing in such a vital site of social production to create contradictions akin to those between capitalist and worker. In view of this, crew members were unhindered from stepping up their production of surpluses and this in turn augured well for an unimpeded growth in the accumulation of capital, a feature that has important implications in the whole process of Africa's (re)development in the current epoch. In the next chapter, we shall be returning to examine this important facet of the cultural milieu in which the African human resource, the continent's most valuable asset, lives and works as we discuss strategies towards Afrocentric development.

Now for a final word on Vercruijsse's research on Ghana's canoe-fishing industry: this sector of the country's fishing economy is literally more productive than the 'public' or 'state' enterprise. It is still not subject to the overarching exigency of the state's supervisory control, and would therefore be said to be occurring in the 'traditional' arena of productive activity in the quaint classification of 'modernisation' theory. Whilst the contradiction between canoe owner and crew is incipient (see above), this is not the case between the fish-traders (or 'fishermen-owners') who were responsible historically for converting canoe fishing into a source of capital accumulation (they buy the bulk of the fish and are in charge of the marketing process) and the big dealers who represent the state and quasi-state/business interests associated with fishing in the 'modern' sector. As Vercruijsse demonstrates, this contradiction arises essentially because of the pre-eminence of these groups in ultimately controlling fish production in Ghana.

Wrestling with a Soothsayer

If one has to reflect with a feeling of immense gratification on the outcome of Vercruijsse's study of Ghana's canoe-fishing, it is because it is in such a judicious utilisation of Africa's human resource for its *sole internal benefit* that not only lies the possibilities of African peoples halting the ceaseless brigandage of the European World in Africa, but even more importantly, ensuring their *survival* as a race on this planet. We cannot over stress the fact that the European World will not 'let go' of Africa voluntarily. It has to be forced to do that by an Africa that withdraws from the contemporary 'world' economy, and embarks on a radically alternative trajectory of (re)development based on African priorities and goals. We shall focus more closely on this in the following chapter.

Just as a study that examines the limitless liberatory capacities of the utilisation of African human labour in an *autocentric* economic production gives cause for celebration, Africa is entitled also to recall with pride another strategic use of its human resource in recent history especially at a time when Western publicists who are feverishly re-writing the accounts of the era wish to pulverise this with a vengeance. In 1968, Henry Kissinger, then professor of government at Harvard University, was appointed presidential advisor on national security by the newly elected president, Richard Nixon. One of the first tasks that Kissinger had was to head a special commission to study the state of the national liberation struggle in Southern Africa. A year later, he completed his study, the so-called NSSM 39.[48] A preamble to its conclusion stated emphatically that the preservation of the vast US/Western economic and strategic interests in the region lay in the effective control of Namibia, Zimbabwe, Mozambique, Angola and, most importantly, South Africa by the immigrant European-minority populations in these countries. The conclusion stressed: 'There is no likelihood in the foreseeable future that [African] liberation movements could overthrow or seriously threaten the existing white governments.'[49] Furthermore, the 'whites are here to stay and the only way that constructive change can come about is through them. There is no hope for the blacks to gain the political rights they seek through violence, which will only lead to chaos and increased opportunities for the communists.'[50] Fundamentally, the assumptions and the conclusions of NSSM 39 were based on the following strategic and racist premises: 'Military realities *rule out a Black victory at any stage. Moreover, there are reasons to question the depth and permanence of Black Resolve.*'[51] (emphasis added)

Invalidation

Less than six years after NSSM 39, Mozambique and Angola were freed by African insurgents, terminating 400 years of the occupation of their homelands by Portuguese colonialism; less than 12 years after NSSM 39, Zimbabwe was freed by African insurgents, terminating nearly 100 years of the occupation of their homeland by British colonialism; less than 20 years after NSSM 39, Namibia was freed by African insurgents, terminating nearly 75 years' occupation of their homeland by South Africa with the connivance of the West; less than 25 years after NSSM 39, the world holds its breath as African peoples are about to liberate South Africa, the most important national liberation struggle currently waged in the world, thus bringing to an end over 300 years of the occupation of their homeland by a myriad of European 'settlers'. No doubt, these historic African successes make nonsense of both the assumptions and the conclusions of Kissinger's study, which we must indicate, broadly guided the US/Western government, economic and financial policies on Southern Africa in the subsequent two decades.

Foundations of Afrocentrism

As African liberation forces in the fields and forests of Southern Africa sought to invalidate the racist assumptions of the soothsayers of eurocentric history, another group of Africans, this time in the closets of their studies, seminar and lecture room, were carrying out another major battle of invalidation. For the African scholar, the epoch of the restoration of independence carried with it the enormous burden of constructing an African historiography that would comprehensively capture the dramatic shifts of fortunes and furloughs that had broadly characterised the development of African history which we sketched earlier on in the first chapter of this book. C.L.R. James, the philosopher of the pan-African liberation movement may have been alluding more poignantly to the taxing nature of this project, rather than the obvious celebratory mood of the occasion when he observes in a preface to one of his works on Africa: 'Except for Southern Africa, a whole continent has gained its independence in less than twenty-five years. I have to insist - and I shall keep on saying it again and again - that I know nothing in history like it...'[52]

Schools and Questions

Apart from a marginal grouping of African scholars which subscribes to an 'Africanised' genre of what is otherwise a eurocentric strain in this task of building up an African historiography (namely, the Mazruian School of the 'Trilaterised' Heritage[53] - of the 'Traditional', which it claims to be under 'decay'; the West and the Arabic, both of which supposedly constitute the sites of a major mortal and multifaceted battle that would determine the fate of Africa), the dominant Schools of African history (Ibadan, Nsukka, Makerere, Dar es Salaam) began to breach, right from the eve of the restoration of independence especially with the 1956 publication of Onwuka Dike's classic *Trade and Politics in the Niger Delta*, those seemingly impregnable contours of the continent's historical landscape which appeared to have frozen African history in the depths of the three 'seasons' of conquest referred to above (see chapter one). Members of these Schools would eventually concentrate their endeavour on the latter two 'seasons' of conquest (Arabic/muslim, the West). They pointedly posed four fundamental questions to aid this crucial work of reconstruction: (a) What was happening in the Africa that is the subject of my research *prior* to the 'season' of conquest? (b) How did this Africa that is the subject of my research *respond* to this 'season' of conquest? (c) What *Africaness* can I reclaim under the encrusted layers of foreign occupations? (d) How does the Africa which is the subject of my research *cope* with this History during the age of the Re-establishment of Independence?

Inevitably, the outcome of these projects varied from School to School, with the regional particularities or peculiarities of the survey helping to accentuate whatever impact researchers would have given to the course of history here and there. Nonetheless, an African historiography, laboriously worked out by Africa's *own* scholars was now taking shape. Except of course, that apart from the section of the historiography that dealt with Africans who lost their independence much later, that is during the third 'season' of conquest, our understanding of the rest of Africa appeared to be

inexorably tainted with the consequences of the second 'season' - the Arab/
muslim invasion.

Cheikh Anta Diop's Scholarship

Thankfully, Africa and African peoples all over the world were spared the
agony of an indefinite wait to resolve this crisis of constructing a
comprehensive African historiography. The breakthrough occurred with
the work of Cheikh Anta Diop, Africa's eminent historian, physicist,
egyptologist, linguist and philosopher.

The central focus of Diop's scholarship is of course Egypt, the Egyptian
civilisation, humanity's first documented civilisation, but the conclusions
that emerge from his near-40 years of research work and publications which
culminated in *Civilization or Barbarism*, radically challenged the orthodoxies
on practically every facet of scholarly discourses - from the origin of the
human species to economic development. Utilising prodigious evidence
from history, philosophy, archaeology and linguistics, Diop shows that
Egypt was a Black civilisation, and that Blacks, *African Peoples*, are the
indisputable heirs to this illustrious heritage. To this effect, Diop demonstrates
that the prevalent eurocentric interpretation of Egypt as a white civilisation
began during the 19th century and was intended to reinforce European
racism and expanding imperialism in Africa and elsewhere in the world.[54]
In contrast, Diop proves through a copious reading of the 'classical' texts,
prior to the eurocentric distortion of Egyptian history, including the records
by Greeks themselves that a long list of what makes up the Who's Who in
Greek science, history and philosophy (Thales, Plato, Eudoxus, Pythagoras,
Democritus, Euclides, Diodorus, Hippocrates, etc.) travelled to Egypt at
various times of their intellectual career and were students of 'black
skinned, woolly-haired' African priests who were the 'true keepers of
scientific knowledge at the time.'[55] 'Thales, who inaugurated the cycle of
being the first to introduce Egyptian science into Greece, particularly
geometry and astronomy... [taught] Pythagoras all he knew [and] advised
him to follow his own example, to go and complete his training with the
Egyptian priests... This is why Pythagoras spent twenty two years in Egypt,
obtaining information about all the sciences that he could; when he returned
to Greece, he founded the sect that bears his name.'[56] And Jamblichus, his
biographer, stresses: 'Pythagoras acquired in Egypt the science for which
he is generally considered to be a scholar.'[57] Thus, through painstaking

scholarship, Diop shows that the Greek civilisation, which is respected as the origin of the European World's intellectual work owes an immense debt to Egypt's astounding achievements.

What therefore is the relevance of this information on African creativity and control of its heritage in antiquity to the African person walking the contemporary stage of history, aimlessly dispossessed, disoriented, distressed and humiliated? If the great Egyptians were 'woolly-haired blacks', so what? Or put it in other words: Why does Diop have to re-construct a 5000-year epochal stretch of African historical experience, or what he aptly terms a 'Sociology of African History'? Firstly, we note right away that Diop subverts the 'constraining' boundaries that had since compartmentalised Africa's history to pale into the overarching dictates of the three 'seasons' of conquest. Suddenly, these 'seasons' become more marginal historical constructs. An African dominant Presence on its homeland, but even more strategically world-wide emerges as a colossus:

> Instead of presenting itself to history as an insolvent debtor, the Black world of theEgyptian is theinitiator of the 'western'civilization flaunted before our eyes today. Pythagoran mathematics, the theory of the four elements of Thales of Miletus, Epicurian materialism, Platonic idealism, Judaism, Islam, and modern science are rooted in Egyptian cosmogony and science. One needs only to meditate on Osiris, the redeemer-god, who sacrifices himself, dies, and is resurrected to save mankind, a figure essentially identifiable with Christ. A visitor to Thebes in the Valley of Kings can view the Moslem inferno in detail (in the tomb of Seti I, of the Nineteenth Dynasty), 1700 years before the Koran. Osiris at the tribunal of the dead is indeed the 'lord' of revealed religions, sitting enthroned on Judgement Day, and we know that certain Biblical passages are practically copies of Egyptian moral texts. Far be it from me to confuse this brief reminder with a demonstration. It is simply a matter of providing a few landmarks to persuade the incredulous Black African reader to bring himself to verify this. To his great surprise and satisfaction, he will discover that most of the ideas used today to domesticate, atrophy, dissolve, or steal his 'soul,' were conceived by his own ancestors.[58]

Yet, Egypt was no isolated African phenomenon, a-flash-in-the-pan in an historical landscape! Egypt emerged from the Ethiopian civilisation, itself evolving 'from the complex interior womb of the African motherland.'[59] The relationship between the Egyptian civilisation and the civilisations that would emerge in the Western Sudan (3000 miles to the West) at the beginning of this millennium, offers Diop the opportunity to contribute to another sphere of Africa's scholarship of reconstruction - this time on the fascinating subject of migration. Diop displays the breath-taking affinity that exists between the west African language of Wolof and that of the ancient Egyptians, no doubt a dramatic reminder to us all that the proud descendants of the pharaohs now walk the streets of Dakar! The similarity between the names of Egyptian gods and cosmogonies and those of the Yoruba and several other nationalities of west Africa for instance, cannot cease to amaze.

What Diop has done is to deploy a rigorous *oeuvre* of discourse that frees the African person forever from the anguish of existence on the politico-economic periphery and psycho-social anonymity in which they have been boxed by conquerors whose impact on human history has only been within very recent epochs. Already, an ever-lengthening string of African World intellectuals working in various disciplines have embarked on this Afrocentric project. It is a painful, but a conscientiously determined task to recast a disgorged inheritance - by situating the African centrally at the site of his or her existence. In 1988, following the publication of her novel, *Beloved*, the African American writer, Toni Morrison told the London *City Limits* in an interview: 'I write in order to enlighten black people, not from the need to explain to others. I don't want people to say what will *they* think about it if you write that way or if we have a movie like this. That means that we are still worrying about what *they* think rather than developing the discipline to communicate with one another. This is about me and you. When I write a book I don't have these people in my mind. I write what I think is of best interest to black people.'[60] (emphasis in the original).

It is this scholarship of *retrieval* and *redirection* that constitutes the grounding of Afrocentrism. Cheikh Anta Diop's scholarship is at once a restoration of Africa to its central role in the development of human history, and the triumph of rigorous scientific enquiry over eurocentricism, and its varying adherents, and hegemonism. As we shall be arguing shortly, Africa must appropriate its creative genius of the past in constructing a totally new civilisation of socio-economic relations to save itself from the quagmire of what increasingly looks like a certain sentence of death by the high priests and judges of the European World's political and financial institutions.

Notes

1. Quoted in Peter Fryer, *Black People in the British Empire*, op.cit., p.36.
2. Ibid.
3. Ibid.
4. Ibid.
5. Ibid., p.37.
6. Ibid.
7. Ibid.
8. Chinua Achebe, *Morning Yet on Creation Day* (London: Heinemann Education Books, 1977), p.72.
9. Roger Tangari, *Politics in Sub-Saharan Africa*, op.cit., p.60.
10. Rodney, op.cit., p.225.
11. Catholic Institute for International Affairs, *South Africa in the 1980s: State of Emergency* (London:CIIR, 1986), p.65.
12. Rodney, op.cit., p.225.
13. *South Africa in the 1980s*, op.cit.
14. See Noam Chomsky, 'The United States: From Greece to El Salvador, in Chomsky, *et al*, *Superpowers in Collision* (Harmondsworth: Penguin Books, 1982), 1982), pp.20-42.
15. Ibid., p.21.
16. Ibid.
17. Quoted in A.N. Porter and A.A. Stockwell, *British Imperial Policy and Decolonisation*, 1938-64 Vol I: 1938-51 (Basingstoke and London: Macmillan, 1987), p.103.
18. Cf. Noam Chomsky, 'Intervention in Vietnam and Central America: Parallels and Differences,' *Monthly Review*, Vol 37, No.4, September 1985, p.5.
19. Claude Ake, *A Political Economy of Africa* (Harlow:Longman, 1981), especially ch. 3 and 5.
20. Rodney, *How Europe Underdevelopment Africa*, op.cit., p.188.
21. Ibid.
22. Bob Fitch and Mary Oppenheimer, *Ghana: End of an Illusion* (New York and London: Monthly Review, 1966), p.42.
23. Ibid., p.44.
24. Ibid., p.42.
25. Ibid., p.44.
26. Bade Onimode, *Imperialism and Underdevelopment in Nigeria: The Dialectic of Mass Poverty* (London: Zed Books, 1982), pp.47-55.

27. R. Olufemi Ekundare, *An Economic History of Nigeria: 1860-1960* (London: Methuen, 1973), p.225.

28. Ibid.

29. Quoted in Onimode, op.cit., p.48.

30. Ibid.

31. Ekundare, op.cit., p.226.

32. Ekundare, op.cit., p.226.

33. Quoted in Okwudiba Nnoli, 'A short history of Nigerian Underdevelopment,' in Nnoli, ed., *Path to Nigerian Development* (Dakar: Codesria, 1981), p.124.

34. Rodney, op.cit., p.188.

35. Ibid.

36. Fitch and Oppenheimer op. cit., p44 .

37. Ibid., p.45.

38. Ibid.

39. Quoted in Ibid., p.44.

40. Emile Vercruijsse, *The Penetration of Capitalism: A West African Case Study* (London and the Hague: Zed Books/Institute of Social Studies: 1984), p.73.

41. Fitch and Oppenheimer, op.cit., p.93.

42. Quoted in Vercruijsse, op.cit., p.79.

43. Walter Rodney, 'The African Revolution,' in Paul Buhle (ed.), op.cit., p.43.

44. Walter Rodney, 'The colonial economy,' in A.Adu Boahen (ed.), op.cit., pp.344-345.

45. Vercruijsse, op.cit., p.5.

46. Ibid., p.154.

47. Ibid., p.155.

48. Ibid., p.155.

49. Ibid., p.155.

50. Ibid., p.105.

51. Ibid., p.90.

52. C.L.R. James, *Nkrumah and the Ghana Revolution* (London: Alison & Busby, 1982), p.8.

53. See, for instance, Ali Mazrui, 'The Reincarnation of the African State: A Triple Heritage in Transition From Pre-colonial Times,' *Presence Africaine* (Paris), Nos 127-128, 3rd and 4th Quarterlies, 1983, pp.114-127 and Mazrui *The Africans: A Triple Heritage* (London : BBC Publications, 1986).

54. Cheikh Anta Diop, *The African Origin of Civilisation*, op.cit., especially ch 2 & 3.

55. Cheikh Anta Diop, *Civilisation or Barbarism* (New York: Lawrence Hill Books, 1991), p.346.
56. Quoted in Ibid.
57. Ibid.
58. Diop, *The African Origin of Civilisation*, op.cit., pp.xiv-xv.
59. Ibid., particularly ch 1,7 and 10.
60. See 'Living Memory,' *City Limits* (London) 31 March-7 April 1988, p.11.

Truth, one would have thought, is not a simple, once-given, God-ordained, immutable entity but more like a combination of sense perception with our scientific concepts, others' testimony and traditional knowledge and custom. As an account of reality which exists independently of our consciousness of it, the truth does not depend on the status or authority of the person rendering it or on the elegance or beauty of our description, but on the extent to which our account conforms with reality, that is, what is the case, and coheres with all existing knowledge. We attain the truth - if and when we ever do - not by confining ourselves to the narrow circle of received or immediate experience only, but through a comprehensive view of interpretation and correlation.

Mokwugo Okoye, 'A Little Heresy', 1975

Chapter 3

African (Re)development: Towards Provincialised Socio-economic Relations

The total world population is [now] 3 billion human beings, while [US citizens] number 200 million. This is a one-to-fifteen odd. If force comes to prevail against right, the US can be taken over, and all that we have will be snatched away by the hungry masses of the world.

- US President Lynden Johnson, 1966

The gap between rich and poor countries is continually widening. As of the 1970s, more than one-half of the world population will be living in independent countries in the southern hemisphere. These people will be hungry and will have access to less than one-tenth of the stock of goods and services produced by mankind... Our security will be directly related to that of the underdeveloped world. Security means development, for without development there will be no security.

- Robert McNamara, US Defence Secretary, 1966; later, president of the World Bank

In 1987, the United States Commission on Demographic Crisis (CDC) published its report on a study it carried out to determine an International Suffering Index. This research focused on most of the world's sovereign states. Utilising a number of socio-economic indices such as population growth, gross national product, infant mortality, illiteracy and food consumption, and measuring these on a 0-10 scale, indicating a deficiency-sufficiency range, the CDC concluded by classifying these states in two main groups: (a) Least Suffering Rates (LSR) - these included the US, the then Soviet Union, Cuba, Britain, the former West Germany and Japan, and (b) Highest Suffering Rates (HSR) - which included Somalia, Ethiopia, Burkina Faso, Central African Republic, Ghana, Mali and Nigeria.

In summarising the outcome of this research, the CDC vice-president, Joseph Spiedel, was quick to stress that the HSR countries were generally those with highest levels of population growth, even though he did not demonstrate how this particular index was related to the rest, except of course to underline how serious a problem it was, reflecting very similar fears expressed 20 years before by the two leading US public figures quoted above. Generally, there was scant analysis in the report of the 'background' political and socio-economic factors which produced these contradictory results. This was clearly a case where empirical indicators, instead of helping to enlighten us in our understanding of social development, further obfuscate reality.

The concern of leading Western officials and institutions on the population of countries in the Southern World acquired a bizarre, if not obscene dimension in 1990 when a racist Conservative party member of the British parliament advocated that condoms should be sent to Bangladesh and the Sudan, as a method of limiting the population growth rate of the two countries, which had just experienced extensive deaths and socio-economic dislocations caused by a cyclone in the former and a crop failure in the latter. It was not evident anywhere in this call for condom-intervention that a lower population growth rate, or indeed a population tally lower than the current number in either of the two countries would have prevented any of the tragedies. In parallel vein, the so-called environmental pressure group, Earth First!, sees the current spread of the AIDs epidemic, and the calamity of famine in a number of African countries as 'the Earth's salvation, ridding the planet of a particularly destructive life-form (human beings).'[1] Earth First! has reinforced its position on the subject by specifically calling for a denial of any external food shipment to the African famine victims because the 'problem of African starvation [is] merely a question of human numbers moving beyond the carrying capacity of the land, and seeing the solution as just a population crash.'[2]

If the above outbursts amount to a silly use of the size of the population of a people as a red herring to explain social phenomenon, or indeed verge on what Rudolph Bahro would describe as 'eco-fascism,'[3] these charges may not be as obvious in the next example. In a special feature article on Africa in the London *Times Literary Supplement* in September 1991, the British historian Roland Oliver notes: 'Africa's population problem by itself offers almost a sufficient explanation of the continent's growing poverty, as compared even with the rest of the [Southern] World. In the 1960s, the annual rate of population growth in Africa was roughly similar to that in Southern Asia and Latin America, at around 2.5 per cent. During the 1970s and 1980s, the Southern Asian and Latin American rates decreased, while that of Africa increased dramatically to 3.5 per cent.'[4] Once again, there is no evidence shown anywhere in this article on how population growth affects, as in this case, what Oliver refers to as Africa's 'growing poverty'. As we shall soon show, the cynical use of population by leading Western publicists to explain the crisis of (re)development in the Southern World is essentially diversionary. It is in fact a continuing effort made by the West to deny its *instrumental* role in creating the barbarism of contemporary Southern political economies. The result has been that whilst the former represents just about 20 per cent of the globe's population, it appropriates nearly nine-tenths of the annual stock of goods and services produced by humanity, to note the converse of the striking revelation made by Robert McNamara on the critical subject of the pattern of the consumption of the world's resources cited in one of the epigraphs at the beginning of this chapter. We shall be arguing later that the subject of African (re)development in the current epoch is only meaningfully discussed within the context of 'provincialised' social praxis which predicates on the cultural essence(s) of African peoples. Before that though, it is pertinent to demonstrate that neither the size of Africa's population nor its rate of growth is an adequate factor in explaining either the drastic fall in Africa's food production, particularly in the last 20 years, or indeed the continent's generalised socio-economic crisis as those vulturous voices of so-called Africanists in the West wish to contend.

The Hijack of Populations

Africa's population is presently about 500 million, a three-fold increase since 1900. Not until the beginning of this century did Africa record an appreciable increase in its population after 300 years of stagnation caused by the mass transportation of millions of its peoples to the Americas/Caribbean to work the mines and plantations, and build the cities and economies of a continent that had just been recently pillaged and conquered by a ruthless European imperialism. Between 1650 (approximately 100 years after the start of this exportation of Africans) and 1850, Africa's population remained roughly at 100 million.[5] This was a period that showed high increases in Europe (from 103 million-274 million) and Asia (257 million-656 million).[6] In the subsequent 50 years, Europe's population increased by about 70 per cent (274 million-423 million), and Asia's increased by about 50 per cent (656 million-857 million).[7] In contrast, Africa's population increased from 100 million-120 million, a rise of 20 per cent.[8]

It was not surprising that the extraordinary increase in Europe's population between 1850 and 1900 coincided broadly with the progress of its conquest across the world, which ultimately created the territorial 'outlet' for its 'excess' human beings. (Indeed between 1820 and 1920, 55 million Europeans emigrated[9] to these conquered lands of the Southern World, particularly the Americas, establishing in effect the highest number of the voluntary movement of a people from one continent to another ever in history.) By 1800, Europe was already claiming the control of 55 per cent of the world's total territorial land space.[10] The significance of this claim is clear because on the eve of the outset of its global conquest, Europe was a little less than 35 per cent of the earth's lands.[11] By 1878, Europe had conquered 67 per cent of these lands,[12] and by 1914, the eve of the major war of its principal powers, it had extended its aggression to cover the occupation of 85 per cent of the world's territory.[13]

As for the increase in Africa's population between 1850-1900, and subsequently during the greater part of this century, namely 400 *years after the start of the holocaust*, it is easy to detect that this development had occurred at an epoch when the 'stability' of the European colonial occupation and exploitation of the African homeland itself required a continually high turnover of the continent's human resources: precisely cheap labour, as we have already shown in this study especially in chapter one. So, these 'surplus' Africans, in this century, have been tied up intrinsically with a totalising economy that produces goods and services for Western consumption. It should not be forgotten, as we have also shown earlier, that several thousands of them died whilst constructing the roads, railways and other infrastructural requirements of the colonial economy, not to mention those who perished digging up minerals in mines or cultivating assorted crops in plantations. Millions in the concentration camps or 'reserves' in east/central/southern Africa had had their lives wrecked, reduced to destitution, and homeless. At least one-half a million conscripts died fighting for the intra-European wars of 1914-1918 and 1939-1945 and tens of thousands others, disabled and demobilised, were abandoned to their fate with scant rehabilitation programmes by the European occupation regimes. But most tragic of all, six million others have died in the numerous conflicts that have raged in 'post'-colonial Africa in the past 33 years which centre principally on whether or not one African nation/nationality or another should belong to states created strategically by Europe to exploit the people and their resources.[14]

While it is true that rapid increases in population growth could affect the food balance in a given human society, an increase in the number of the hungry and/or starving is *not* a direct consequence of population growth. Africa's current population is, for instance, less than one-half that of China's which is 1.5 billion. While anything between 60-75 per cent of Africans are malnourished, less than 5 per cent of Chinese could be categorised as such. Indeed in a related example shown in a recent study of India, Mark Tully, one of the very few non-eurocentric Western publicists working in the Southern World contrasts the Indian crisis of (re)development with that in China as follows: 'There are countries which are poorer than India, but there is none which has so many poor people. Those who are now talking of the victory of freedom should perhaps ponder that strange fact that one of the freest countries in the world, which has made an all-out effort since independence to eradicate its legacy of poverty, has been much less successful than its communist neighbour. Of course India's achievements in some fields are more impressive than China's, but the fact remains that communism has provided better education, better health services and more food than democracy has.'[15]

Capacities Despite Holocaust

Britain's total land mass is 244,755 sq. km. This is roughly the size of Uganda which is 236, 860sq. km., but far less than one-thousandth of Africa's land mass. Yet Britain's population of 56 million is more than four times that of Uganda and is just under eight times less than the whole of Africa's. Eighty per cent of Uganda's arable land, some of the richest in Africa remains uncultivated. Were Uganda to expand its current food production by just 50 per cent, not only would it be completely self-sufficient, but it would be able to feed the states contiguous to its territory without difficulty.

The overall statistics of the African situation is even more revealing as with regards to the continent's long-term possibilities. Just a quarter of the potential arable land of Africa is being cultivated presently.[16] (Even here, an increasingly high proportion of the cultivated area is assigned to the so-called cash crops for exports to the West.) *and the rest of this uncultivated arable land represents 66 per cent of the entire world's potential.*[17] Africa constitutes a spacious, rich and arable land mass that can support its population, which is still one of the world's least densely distributed, into the indefinite future. But there is only one condition for the attainment of this goal - *Africa must utilise these immense resources for the express benefits of its peoples.* In the contemporary political economic relations, Africa's resources are used largely to support the West, and an overseer grouping of local social forces which appears to exist solely to police the dire straits of existence that is the lot of the average African. It is in studying the varying perspectives of the nature of these relations that we can have a greater understanding of Africa's (re)development possibilities rather than the eurocentric preoccupations with the continent's population or its growth rate. Neither attribute accounts for the current emergency.

History's Long Shadow

It cannot be over-stressed that Western imperialism dehumanised and radically distorted the African society, particularly its rich agricultural heritage which had singularly been at the core of the varying facets and sites of its civilisation which emerged 5000 years ago. Indeed the African civilisation represents humanity's earliest evidence of not only the extensive domestication of a natural environment, but also the construction of several advanced political economies as the examples of Kush, Nubia, Ethiopia, Egypt, Ghana, Zimbabwe, Yoruba and Igbo show. Yet, as we highlighted earlier on in this study, this mid-millennium European invasion of Africa, with its concomitant genocides, exportation of peoples (slave trade), and finally occupation (colonialism), was the culmination of an invasion process that began earlier on in the millennium by the Arab/muslim attack of the continent. As from the 7th, through to the 12th century, Arab/muslim armies swept across most of the north of the continent, vandalising, confiscating and ultimately occupying about one-third of Africa, from the Red Sea to the north-west Atlantic coast, which they still occupy to this day. In this context, the Arab/muslim invasion directly paved the way to Europe's subsequent attack. As should be expected, the effect on Africa of this millennium of conquest and occupation has been conspicuously ruinous. Africa is ravaged by this holocaust. Its peoples, at home, and the diaspora in Europe, the Americas/Caribbean and elsewhere, are still striving to recover. As we showed in the last chapter, the essential character of Europe's initial control of Africa remains despite the latter's struggle for the restoration of independence from the occupation, which began in the 1950s. The overwhelming majority of Africa's productive labour continues to produce goods and services for export to the West. The average African labour is strategically deployed in either of the following two crucial spheres of economic activities: (a) 'cash crop' farming, to refer to the apparently meaningless term of Western 'development studies', where it cultivates crops such as palm produce, cotton, cocoa, coffee and groundnuts for export to the West, or (b) working deep in the gold, diamond, tin, copper and bauxite mines and petroleum oil fields, where it extracts the mineralogical riches of the continent, again for export to the West. Except in very isolated cases, no African leadership in this epoch of the restoration of independence has seriously questioned Africa's continuing role as a primary producer of 'cash crop' and mineral resources for the Western economies, a fact that underlines the urgency of the insight made in the frontispiece to the last chapter by Chinua Achebe, Africa's leading novelist.

Capital Net Exporter

Yet, it is not within this historically familiar terrain of the exogenous existentialism of the African productive labour that the violence of contemporary Western exploitation of Africa is acutely felt. Rather, it is at that site of economic 'relations' with the Southern World which Western 'development studies', and its pervasive and suffocating cultural propaganda output, always assigned to the exclusive role of the West - namely the provider of capital for development, or more appropriately (*re*)development. So, the news that will surely astound, if not shock the limpid perceptibility of a world that has been nurtured by the West to believe the contrary, is that Africa, along with the other two continents of the South, is a *net* exporter of capital to the West. The grim statistics of the past decade provide screaming evidence of the burden of dispossessiveness which Africa is presently forced to carry by the West.

In 1981, Africa recorded a net capital export of US$5.3 billion to the West.[18] In 1985, this figure shot up to US$21.5 billion.[19] It is very important to emphasise Africa's 1985 net capital transfer to the West because it was the same year that the world was confronted with the depressing television pictures which reported the unfolding tragedy of the Ethiopian famine. The Irish pop musician, Bob Geldof, launched his 'Live Aid' Africa Famine charity programme in response to the tragedy, with a globally-televised pop fiesta that raised US$75 million. Such was the popularity of Geldof in the West that the then Irish government lobbied strongly for him to be awarded the Nobel Prize for Peace in 1985. A number of observers at the time reckoned that Geldof narrowly missed the prize, but he was knighted by the British government as well as receiving other official commendations elsewhere in the West. But what was the prize for Africa that transferred the thundering sum of US$21.5 billion *in excess* to the West that year? The Burden Prize for Western Wealth? Still on the Geldof 'Live Aid' pop extravaganza, it should be recalled that a special study carried out by John Clarke for the charity organisation, Oxfam, concluded poignantly: 'For every £1 given in famine relief to Africa in 1985, the West reclaimed some £2 in debt payments.'[20]

Three years later, the crisis of Africa's dispossessiveness worsened. Africa's net capital export to the West in 1988 hit the phenomenal level of US$36 billion.[21] In other words, for *each day* in 1988, Africa's net capital transfer to the West was US$100 million. By 1992, the levels of this African daily dispatch of value to the West had increased even further as its net capital transfer for that year hit a new threshold: US$50 billion.[22] It should be stressed that none of the figures quoted above includes the national accounting of the Arab states of north Africa nor that of South Africa. They only refer to that geo-political part of the continent that Western social sciences and financial institutions categorise as 'sub-Saharan Africa'.It is no doubt instructive for any serious student of Africa-West 'relations' to reflect carefully on the multifaceted consequences on Africa of this (now) regularised net capital export to the West, because this is the continent whose humanity is routinely derided in the Western media and academia as a bunch of incompetents, helpless, hungry and beggars.

Two-thirds of this net capital export from Africa, as well as those from the rest of the South, are for 'servicing' the debt which the West claims that Africa owes it. Southern countries now allocate 40-50 per cent of their increasingly depreciating earnings from the sale of agricultural and mineralogical commodities produced for Western consumption to pay for what some scholars have dubbed this late 20th century 'tribute.'[23] The virtual collapse during the course of the past two decades of the prices of these products is a subject that has been comprehensively discussed in the recent excellent study by leading Southern World economists, *The Challenge to the South*, which was commissioned by the South Commission and from where the following figures are derived.[24] Apart from petroleum oil, the prices of 33 principal commodities produced in the South in 1988 were 30 per cent less in actual terms than the average during the period 1979-81. This slump in prices was worse in food and tropical beverages which was 37 per cent. As for petroleum oil, the fall was 64 per cent. Predictably, the terms of trade between the South and the West fell sharply by 1988 as a result of this development: by 29 per cent, if compared to the figures of 1980, or even by 49 per cent if the Southern countries were primarily petroleum oil exporters. But what was more serious from this deterioration of trade between the South and the West was the impact it had on the extent of capital transfer from the former to the latter. It makes chilling reading indeed, but should be quoted at some length here:

> ... taking 1980 levels of exports and prices as a base, for the eighteen main non-oil commodities exported by developing countries it amounted to nearly [US] $83 billion between 1981 and 1986... To put these figures in a longer perspective, the average real price of non-oil commodities for the whole period 1980-88 was 25 per cent below that of the previous two decades and the terms of trade of non-oil developing countries were 8 per cent below those of the 1960s and 13 per cent below those of the 1970s.[25]

Unlike the period of 'classical' colonialism, this 'tribute' from Africa, and the South, is exacted without requiring the presence of a Western-occupying regime on the ground. Presently, African governments carry out this task for the West, and the process has been unrelentlessly ruthless on the peoples as the current socio-economic situation in Africa attests. Quite clearly, the West has never had it so good.

Just Who Owes Whom What?

The mere notion of Africa owing the West anything is to say the least ludicrous, given the West's continuing pillaging of Africa for nearly 500 years now. This is surely an Orwellian use of language that is only intelligible within the contours of a Western-hegemonic reading of the 'relationship' among the world's peoples and nations. So, according to the 'international' financial institutions such as the IMF and the World Bank, effectively run and controlled by the West, Africa's current debt to the West is about US$300 billion, and this represents 100 per cent of the continent's gross national product.[26] It is calculated that by the year 2000, this debt would hit the US$550 billion mark if the current trend in (Western) bank rates continues,[27] but by then Africa would have paid off the West at least ten times the original principal just on debt 'servicing'.

A brief comparative note on another Southern continent will highlight the other features of the African crisis which are not often obvious in the labyrinth of 'international' financing statistics. Latin America's own supposed debt to the West is thrice as much as Africa's at US$900 billion. But unlike Africa, the Latin American debt represents just 46 per cent of its gross national product,[28] underlining the severity of the dispossessiveness of the former in relative terms. Moreover two-thirds of Africa's so-called debt is owed to governments (Western) and financial institutions (for instance the IMF and the World Bank), instead of private banks which account for at least 50 per cent of Latin America's. As a result, Africa is under greater pressure to meet its debt 'obligations' than Latin America because in contrast to the private banks, the 'constitutions' of Africa's main 'creditors' don't easily allow for capital rescheduling. This is the background to the West's blanket enforcement of its punitive 'structural adjustment programme' on most African countries, which in recent years has accelerated the *decapitalisation* of these economies. For a final remark on the comparative experience of Latin America, a return to the net export capital accounting for 1985 is relevant. In that year, Latin America's net capital transfer to the West was twice that of Africa's in real terms - US$42.4 billion.[29] But calculated as a proportion of that same year's revenue derived from foreign earnings for the sale of its export products, Africa's net export capital to the West was generally 20-30 per cent higher than that of Latin America. Thus seen from the perspective of the non-uniformity, or the varying impact of the crisis of Western dispossession of the South on two of its three key regional tributaries, instead of the Roland Oliver hallucinatory construct on population referred to earlier on in this chapter, it is easy to understand why Africa's share of the burden appears more desperate than Latin America's.

There is a way that a sudden focus on the configuration of political power in contemporary Africa still creates problems for comprehension, especially in relation to the all too familiar tragedy of existence that is Africa. For 33 years now, almost all of Africa has been led by local political leadership. In essence, these leadership presently oversee this phase of the crisis of African dispossessiveness that has been the subject of this study. These leadership must know of the crisis and its grave ramifications. After all, the quote above on Africa's projected 'debt' to the West by the year

2000 came from no other than an African head of state - President Robert Mugabe of Zimbabwe, in a speech in 1989 whilst visiting London. These leadership must know from the sordid trail of history that links African peoples and the West, that the latter *will always* exploit Africa given the opportunity. It has taken eight generations of Western governments to accomplish their control of Africa, and no future government there would voluntarily abandon such a lucrative harvest of conquest. For a typical Western government therefore, the West's continuing control of African resources does not cease to be an ontological preoccupation.

The African leadership must also know that what 'international' financial institutions describe as the 'African debt to the West' is bogus. *Africa owes the West nothing.* On the contrary, Western debt to Africa, and its peoples around the world run into trillions and trillions of dollars since the 15th century, and it must be paid - someday. If the African leadership know all this, the question still remains: Why do they persist in playing the role of overseer? Just what is the gain for administering so ruthlessly an economy that principally serves the interest of the Western World? Personal financial gains? Family financial gains? Why are the African leadership currently mortgaging the very survival of their own peoples by *authorising* the transfers of critical resources to the West day in, day out?

'Marionettes'

In 1991, the African leadership lost an historic opportunity to confront head-on the seriousness of this crisis. This was during the 1991 summit conference of the Organisation of African Unity in Nigeria which, significantly, attracted more heads of state and government than any other similar gatherings in the past decade. That summit would have been worth the efforts and the millions of Nigerian naira spent on it,[30] considering the harsh socio-economic climate of the times, if the African leadership had renounced these 'debts' as fraudulent. They should then have called for the setting up of a *genuine* international tribunal of adjudicators to look into the *entirety* of Africa-West 'relations' since the 15th century and conclude definitively on precisely who owes whom what. Both sides must declare their willingness to accept the outcome of the tribunal prior to the start of its work.

The African leadership at the summit should also have declared their intention to embark on the utilisation of their resources, human and material, for the express purposes of *their own* (re)development. Of course these 'marionettes' on the historical stage of international politics, to quote, once again, from Chinua Achebe's observation in the frontispiece to the previous chapter of this book, did not attempt whatsoever to create the autonomous space of existence necessary to chart the trajectory of liberation which encapsulates the point made above on the 'debt', nor the demand for the use of Africa's resources for internal purposes only. The African leadership must now realise that they constitute the *immediate* source of the emergency that Africa faces presently. *They bear the primary responsibility.* As we have shown, the West will always wish to exploit Africa. It does not have any other choice, except of course, it is stopped. African leadership have that capability. In this sense, it is too charitable for Achebe to describe these leadership as 'marionettes,' for this implies a grouping which is just being manipulated, without any thought process to break loose from its creator; in other words, an actor without a choice. Stretched to its logical implication, the 'marionette' is left off the hook of responsibility. But the African leadership are no longer lucky, if ever they thought so, that African peoples will come to the conclusion that the former have been bereft of choices to manoeuvre the continent out of this quagmire. The African leadership know what the stakes and conditions are, and they clearly have the choice to stop transferring the continent's resources to the West. It is immensely difficult to envisage any conclusion of an account of the current African tragedy that does not note the role of the African leadership as *active* participants in this epoch of the West's impoverishment of rich Africa.

Illustrating with Nigeria

These questions of 'choice' and 'responsibility' need further elaboration especially empirically. The example of Nigeria could not have been more appropriate in the circumstances, as it was the country in the 1970s which singularly had the resources, both human and material, to transform for the first time in recent history, an African community into one that would be the envy of all African peoples across the world. To underline the optimism of the times, General Olusegun Obasanjo, who was one of the heads of state at the time and who recently ran unsuccessfully for the post of the United Nations secretary general, told his countrymen and women: 'Nigeria will become one of the ten leading nations in the world by the end of the century.'[31]

What follows here is just a summary statement to illustrate the possibilities of 'choice' and 'responsibility' available to an African leadership. Readers interested in a more detailed discussion of the contemporary Nigerian political economy could refer to a recent book on the subject.[32] Federal Nigeria began the year 1970 with unprecedented confidence and vitality. Its mid-January defeat of the Biafran independence movement in the east of the country brought to an end a 30-month old war which had caused the death of 2.5 million people, the overwhelming majority of whom were Biafrans. The 12 million Biafrans who survived the war became a mass pool of refugees overnight in a homeland whose economy had been virtually destroyed. For them, the task of rehabilitation and the reconstruction of a battered heritage was daunting indeed.

The federal government's own priority in the east's economic reconstruction was essentially focused on the region's petroleum oil industry, which constitutes at least two-thirds of Nigeria's production source and capacity. Ironically, there was little damage done to this particular industry as federal war-time strategy was to seize most of the oil wells, refinery and associated facilities almost intact from Biafran control within the first 12 months of fighting (most of the Biafra War was fought out in the central provinces of Biafra, or the so-called Igbo heartland). Reconstruction here therefore meant carrying out urgent maintenance work on a number of oil installations, and the restoration of pipelines destroyed by retreating Biafran forces, two objectives which, incidently, the federals had embarked upon since June 1968 following their capture of the refinery town of Port Harcourt from the Biafrans. (In the 1966/67 production year, prior to the war, the average daily rate of oil output was 418,000 barrels, and by 1969, as a result of the initial phase of federal restoration work in war damaged installations, this increased to 540,000 barrels per day. By the end of 1971, that daily output was averaging 1.5 million barrels.[33]) The end of the war also meant that the foreign technical staff in the industry (mostly British, Americans and Dutch) who left the country in 1967 could now return safely to their posts.

Apart from the 1968/69 fall in federal export earnings from oil due to Biafra's control of the principal production provinces (N29.6 million - 29.6 million naira -, compared to N41 million in 1967/68[34]), Lagos's income from this product shot up dramatically in subsequent years: N75.4 million in 1969/70,[35] N176.4 million during 1970/71,[36] and N603 million in 1971/ 72,[37] the first full year period of uninterrupted production after the war, all underscoring the immense financial gains that accrued to the federal treasury in the wake of the rehabilitation of the eastern petroleum enterprise.

By 1974, Nigeria's export receipts from petroleum was N5 billion, and five years later, this income doubled to N10.4 billion,[38] accounting for about 98 per cent of total earnings. For Nigeria, and indeed the rest of the countries of Africa, except of course the Arab states in the north of the continent and possibly the European minority population-controlled South Africa, this huge financial windfall was unprecedented in 'post'-colonial Africa. And to underline the historical significance of this fiscal development, it should be pointed out that Nigeria's oil income in 1974 alone was more than twice the amount of the total fixed investment it had planned to implement during its 1962-68 first post-independence National Development Plan (about N2.4 billion - even here, at least 50 per cent of the funding was expected from abroad), and just short of twice the N3.2 billion revised investment earmarked for the 1970-74 Second National Development Plan.[39] This evidently sharp contrast in the fortunes of a country, within just a decade, was further illustrated in March 1975 when Nigeria declared that its envisaged investment programme in the Third National Development Plan (1975-80) was at least N42 billion.[40] By this time, calculated on the basis of its gross national product which was US$22.4 billion, Nigeria had emerged as Africa's third richest state, after South Africa and Egypt.[41] The prospects for its future socio-economic development could not have looked more promising than at any time since the 1960 re-establishment of the people's independence, following the termination of the British occupation.

Squandering of Riches[42]

In all the three Nigerian national development plans referred to above, but in particular the second and third which were drawn up during the early 1970s' boom in the oil industry, there was a recurrence of three dominant themes in the set objectives of successive governments involved, to transform the political economy of the Nigerian state: [43] (a) to construct a united, strong and self-reliant country; (b) to construct a just and egalitarian society, with bright and full opportunities for all its citizens, and (c) to construct a free and democratic society. The phenomenal levels of oil sales' receipts provided the financial muscle to accomplish these tasks. Indeed in

1974, a leading government official proclaimed to the world that 'Nigeria's problem was not lack of money, but how to spend the "petro-naira".'[44] Indeed there were hardly any constraints in Nigerian government circles to 'spend the "petro-naira"' windfall during the period, except that none of the three lofty targets cited above was achieved in the process. It was doubtful that any of the three military regimes in power then genuinely pursued any of these stated goals as a task to be accomplished. Their record, which left the economy in a very serious crisis on the eve of the return to civilian government in 1979, underscores this fact.

This was a period of unrelenting corruption in government as top officials lurched ravenously into the public purse in a frenzy. Regional military governors and commanders converted their local administrative units into fiefdoms of elaborately institutionalised nepotism. The business-people who the military had contracted to buy arms during the Biafra War, became millionaires overnight, and expanded their range of commercial interests even further in this post-war squandermania as they secured access to lucrative ventures to construct new military bases, sports facilities, expanded infrastructural development (especially the building of new roads), and new towns, each characterised by enormously-inflated financial returns which were shared mutually with government officials responsible for the contract (these businesspeople would emerge later on in Nigerian politics as principal financiers of the National Party of Nigeria - the party that formed the civilian government at the beginning of the Second Republic in 1979).[45] In one such contract, which would be described easily as far-fetched if it were part of the plot of a children's pantomime, a stadium to be constructed in central Nigeria was initially contracted for N5 million by the local government authorities, but this sum was soon increased dramatically by six-fold to N31 million, but without any economic justification. A prompt local press and public outcry that followed forced the hand of the authorities on the issue, and the latter had to announce that the stadium would now be built for N15.5 million![46] - again, without any economic justification rendered.

There are two other spheres of the financial recklessness of the era that require mention. The first concerned the staging of innumerable festivals by the regimes at tremendous cost to the treasury. The 1977 arts festival, FESTAC, cost the country N600 million, even though some other sources claimed that this was probably twice if not thrice as much,[47] while the international trade fair of the previous year cost N100 million.[48] Secondly, the regimes were too keen to display what was essentially an infantile generosity in handing out packages of money to several foreign governments and institutions. Between 1970 and 1975, the Nigerian government spent at least N50 million in supporting various socio-economic projects, or making outright donations to countries which included Grenada, Somalia, Algeria and Swaziland.[49] These financial offers were usually made whilst the Nigerian head of state was an official visit to the country in question, a trend that was very typical of General Yakubu Gowon.

The stage had now been set for the corruption and profligacy which were the hallmarks of successive military regimes during the course of a decade, a legacy that was 'bequeathed' to the Shehu Shagari presidency when it was sworn into office in 1979 to head the Second Republic's first national government. State officials, either at local or national levels saw the public treasuries as fortune houses to enrich themselves and members of their families. Personal enrichment, party and regional patronage became crucial indices for the quest for, or retention of high office. Not surprisingly, by the end of Shagari's first term as president in July 1983, leading figures of his party, the National Party of Nigeria, were undisguised millionaires, and the Western press had even described one of the president's closest aides, living abroad, as a billionaire.[50] Corruption, graft and greed could not have been so blatantly institutionalised in the workings of a country's economy.[51] The mathematician and social critic Edwin Madunagu correctly describes the era as the 'political economy of state robbery.'[52]

The Shagari regime presided over the most serious economic crisis that Nigeria had faced in 20 years. When it came to power, the country's external reserves, earned mostly from export of petroleum products stood at US$7.5 billion. By 1983, after its first term in office, and the year that it was overthrown by another grouping within the military, these reserves had been virtually eliminated - less than US$1 billion left. Industrial production came almost to a halt because of the inability of enterprises to import raw material and spare parts. In the agricultural sector, the situation was equally dismal. Prices of staple foods rose by over 500 per cent between 1979 and 1981, as agricultural output slumped. This was a country which had been largely self-sufficient in food production 20 years before. Then, agriculture had contributed two-thirds of total export earnings. Since the early 1970s, however, successive governments had begun to depend heavily on petroleum as the main foreign-exchange earner (accounting presently for about 92 per cent of Nigeria's export revenue). A neglect of agricultural production ensued and by the end of 1983, its contribution to the gross domestic product stood at a paltry eight per cent. This was so despite the gigantic expenditure of about US$2.4 billion which the regime claimed that it had devoted to its so-called Green Revolution venture.

The standard of living of the people generally deteriorated during the Shagari presidency. As the slump in agricultural production intensified, there was an unprecedented increase in rural migration to the urban areas, and this brought serious strains on urban facilities, particularly housing, health care and schools. By December 1983, thousands of workers in urban employment across the country were owed salaries and wages in arrears of between 6 and 18 months. This was in spite of the regime's grudging 'concession' in 1980 of a minimum wage of N120 per month (about US$150 per month) instead of the N300 per month demanded by the Nigerian Labour Congress. In contrast to this 'starvation' wage for workers, the regime placed its political public officials on bloated salaries, supplemented by the usual perks such as free housing facilities and maintenance, an annual foreign exchange allowance, free travel, free health care and free tuition for children. Transnational corporations, principally British and of the United States, which still maintain a stranglehold on the Nigerian economy, benefitted enormously from the Shagari regime's profligate fiscal policy, especially its concessional tax offers for business enterprises. Despite the deteriorating economic situation, these foreign firms recorded huge profits whilst progressively paying less taxes. Even after General Buhari's military coup in December 1983, transnational corporations' profits continued to maintain a steady rise despite the downturn in the economy. The results in 1984 for six leading commercial and trading companies indicate that pre-tax profits (as a proportion of turnover) averaged 6.8 per cent as against 3.9 per cent in 1983.[53] Figures for the performance of the giant United Africa Company in the first nine months of 1984 show that while its turnover was down 17 per cent at N596 million compared to the same period in 1983, its profits had more than doubled to N65.9 million.[54]

The Babanginda regime's so-called Structural Adjustment Programme ('SAP'), a plan that was in fact initiated by the IMF, heightened the convulsive stresses in the Nigerian economy. Within the first year of the 'SAP', the naira had been devalued by 75 per cent in relation to the United States dollar, and by mid-May 1990, the devaluation was 90 per cent.[55] This drastic fall in the value of the naira had been maintained, thanks to a

'Second-Tier Foreign Exchange Market' ('SFEM'), a crucial component of the operations of the 'SAP'. 'SFEM' was literally a weekly public auction of a predetermined amount of foreign currencies (principally United States dollar) made available by the country's Central Bank, which in turn set the value of the naira for that week.[56] In practice, this entailed the Central Bank inviting authorised dealers to make a bid for three to five per cent of the foreign currencies on offer.[57] The highest bids of course cleared the stock of the currencies available, but it was the lowest bid made during the transaction that determined the exchange rate of the naira with respect to the dollar for that week.[58] Translated to its *real* buying power locally, which had been compounded by the accompanying steep prices of imports (despite the regime's trade 'liberalisation' policy, an important feature of 'SAP'), as well as those of locally-produced goods and services, the value of the Nigerian naira in mid-May 1990 had fallen by 1000 per cent of its worth in 1986, or prior to the inauguration of the 'structural adjustment programme'.[59]

Commissioned agents, speculators, and various businesses operating in the country, particularly Western corporations, have, as should be expected, cashed in on the immense opportunities created by the floatation of the naira to step up the transfer of capital from Nigeria to overseas, which, as usual, is of course the West. This transfer, coupled with the massive annual export of capital involved in the servicing of Nigeria's 'debt' owed to Western creditors has reinforced the trend in the past 20 years during which the movement of capital has consistently registered a net dividend in favour of the West. (While the Babangida regime thought that it could reduce the proportion of the annual receipts of export trade allocated to so-called external debt servicing from the approximately 50 per cent level during the regime of Buhari's, his predecessor, it has however been the case that as a result of the incessant depreciation of the naira, the continuing fall of commodity prices set by Western markets, and the ever increasing bank rates in the West, Nigeria's 'debt' servicing-export receipts ratio continues to be about 50 per cent in real term.)

Trade 'liberalisation' has ensured the flooding of the Nigerian market with imported goods from the West, which increased by 8.1 per cent in the first year of 'SAP' (from N5.5 billion in 1985 to N6 billion in 1986[60]). But with an ever-weakening naira, the cost of these goods has remained generally prohibitive to most consumers even where many categories have become cheaper than locally produced ones. In some regions of the country, famine and starvation are steadily setting in. In a survey carried out in mid-1987 by the University of Ibadan, and the federal ministry of health, it was found that 2000 children died every day across the country as a result of malnutrition, chronic undernourishment or starvation and related diseases.[61] The survey showed that three in ten children born in the urban areas died before their fifth birthday, while the rate of mortality over the same period in the rural areas was 100 per 1000 live births.[62]

Following a visit to Nigeria in August 1989 to assess the social costs of the 'SAP', three years after its operation, Andrew Buckoke, in an article in the London *Times*, not inauspiciously entitled 'Austerity bites as Nigeria scrapes oil barrel,' writes: 'Nigerians, who have suffered a drop of up to 80 per cent in real incomes, talk of being "sapped"... People discuss the relative merits of "zero-one-zero" or "zero-zero-one", in considering the advisability of having lunch or supper when they can only afford one meal a day.'[63] And elsewhere, Alexander Cockburn observes: 'Between 1985 and 1987, its [Nigeria's] per capita income was halved, from [US]$800 to [US]$380. As a result, the World Bank revised its classification of Nigeria from a middle-income to a low-income country.'[64] So, Nigerians whose leadership boasted 20 years ago that the country's 'problem was not lack of money, but how to spend the "petro-naira",' are currently scraping to survive on barely one meal a day. In effect, the 'Structural Adjustment Programme' is nothing other than a social asphyxiation project.

Undoubtedly, what the Nigerian example shows is the performance of a string of African leadership, *endowed with the resources*, the existence of which they fully acknowledged, that could have been easily used to radically transform the living conditions of their people, but whose choice of action instead hemmed into a megalomaniac disposition to deprive their society of this 'new found' wealth. As was expected, the main depository of these squandered riches was the West. In the 1970s, Nigerians in the West were usually called the 'Arabs of the African World', an obscene reference to the millions of 'petro-naira' which influential members of the Nigerian leadership had invested in Western stocks, shares, bonds and real estate. In contrast, Nigerians here, but particularly those in Europe, are now, in the 1990s, called the 'Turks of the African World', a derogatory reminder of the low-paid jobs and the awfully-squalid conditions at work and housing facilities to which thousands of especially recently-arrived immigrants are subjected.

The Post-Post-Colonial: (Re)development as Survival

It would appear that Roland Oliver, the British historian whose *Times Literary Supplement* article on Africa we referred to earlier on in this chapter, had Nigeria in mind, particularly on the issue of 'accountability' (?), when he concluded his essay by noting: 'With its overriding population problem, Africa can hardly expect to achieve First World standards of economic development within the next century, but with just a little more day-to-day accountability, it could at least recover the confidence to continue the uphill struggle with more success.'[65] Ignoring the gratuitous racism and paternalism evident in this quote, this is yet another indication of Western scholarship on Africa trapped in its eurocentric den, unable to deal seriously with the issues at stake. The day any African government becomes more *accountable* to its public, its peoples (if that indeed is what Oliver means by accountability), then this will constrict the space, and history, which creates the Olivers of the Western World to even dare comment on the African historical and political process. The day *all* of African governments become *accountable* to their peoples, then the Olivers of the Western World and their stock in trade will be rendered irrelevant, just chaffs of narrative digressions.

Just like Nigeria, the whole of Africa 'works' - in the sense that the humanity of this continent has not *ceased* to create wealth for the West despite the obvious deterioration of local social existence. If Western publicists who write (or broadcast) on Africa, and who can literally pick up the latest information on any perspectives of Africa-West 'relations'(including the state of Africa's net capital transfer to the West and the nature of the ever-deteriorating terms of its trade with the latter), by merely tapping a key on a computer keyboard on their desk, do ignore to tell the world the truth about this present phase of the European World crimes in Africa, rather than acting out their now well-known response to the crisis (namely the almost overwhelming conspiracy of silence to confront the core tenets of the subject at stake whilst lurching instead into a megalomaniac drive to dehumanise the African victim), then the important question that inevitably arises from this is: Why is the Western intelligentsia silent on what is clearly a diliberate policy by its regimes, transnational businesses and finance corporations to destroy the very basis of life in Africa? Furthermore, why is the Western intelligentsia *collaborating* in this process of Western genocide in Africa, on the eve of a new millennium, by absolving the criminals and demonising the victim? (For instance, in Britain, lately, such epithets as 'savagery', 'dark continent', 'darkening continent' have been used quite liberally in captions and actual reportage in a number of feature articles, reviews and broadcasts dealing with African issues particularly in the so-called liberal publications/radio/television including *Times Higher Education Supplement, Times Literary Supplement, The Times, The Independent, The Guardian, BBC Radio 4,* and *BBC Television 1* and *2.* The inclusion of *The Guardian* in this frenzy of racist reporting on Africa is no doubt significant because this is a journal that has always prided itself as the 'most liberal' of the British 'liberal' newspapers. Indeed, its in-house 'expert' on Africa and doyenne of 'African Reporting' in the British press, Victoria Brittain, did not wish to be left out in this British 'darkening' craze of the age to dehumanise African peoples as ritualistically as possible in the media, when she captioned a *Guardian* 13 February 1993 article on Africa 'Donors fail dark continent'.)

There are of course epistemological, if not historical problems inherent in some of the key assumptions in both questions above, one of which is that this intelligentsia has either been neutral or uninvolved in the saga of Western criminality on African peoples and others across the world during the past five centuries. On the contrary, the Western intelligentsia has never played such a lofty, humanist role in this gory history as we have shown again and again in this book. David Dabydeen reminds us elsewhere[66] that besides the obvious state operatives of the day, namely the politician, the soldier and the merchant, the European conquest of the world was the *work* of its intelligentsia - the poet, the novelist, the anthropologist... So, the two questions posed above appear utterly preposterous! Given its role in history, what would have been a surprise, a pleasant one for that matter, was if the Western intelligentsia was behaving otherwise in its response to the European World's current thieving enterprise in Africa. As Malcolm X, the cerebral African American revolutionary noted in very comparable circumstances 30 years ago, the Western person of ideas would not walk along the liberatory route of human responsibility to denounce Europe's crimes on the African precisely 'because every time he sees [the African] face he sees a mirror of his crime - and his guilt conscience can't bear to face it.'[67] As the West squeezes Africa further, extracting as much of the continent's wealth that it can lay its hand on in the coming months and years, its intelligentsia can therefore be expected to intensify its frantic hatched job of covering up every available trace of blood in the murder scene.

To return finally to Roland Oliver's essay in the *Times Literary Supplement,* it is now obvious to state that no African peoples, even including the leadership which transfer Africa's wealth to the West, as the Nigerian example acutely demonstrates, have ever sought to achieve 'First World standards of economic development' - whatever these mean. Surely, whatever these 'standards' are, they would have been established or achieved within the crucibles of a particular cultural environment, dictating its needs, goals and priorities. They are therefore *not* universal or necessarily exportable, even if the initial resources for the construction of this development process may have come from another environment -from Africa, in the Western case, as we have shown in this study. What is not often clear in the minds of Western publicists such as Roland Oliver is that Africans don't envy the West's 'standards of economic development,' and its role in the world. They are instead *outraged* because Africa provided, and *still* provides the critical resources for the maintenance of the West's power position. What Africans want from the West is quite simple: Leave Us Alone. The Olivers of the West whose scholarship gives the 'intellectual' cover to the buccaneering enterprise of their governments and transnational companies in Africa must have to apologise openly to generations of dispossessed Africans or learn gracefully to shut up! Africa has nothing *whatsoever* that is humanistic to learn from the West. Contrariwise, African peoples' experience with the European World has always been a crippling exposure to the latter's variegated policy of 'creeping' genocide: enslavement of millions of Africans for 300 years; millions of Africans working its plantations and mines without payment for 300 years; millions of Africans building up its cities and towns without payment for 300 years; seizure of the African homeland for up to 400 years, in some cases; jettisoning millions of Africans onto the concentration camps of 'reserves' here and there; converting millions of Africans into a cheap reservoir of labour to grow assorted 'cash crops' for the consumption of its population, and dig up mines for strategic minerals required by its industry; its current kleptomaniac *decapitalisation* of the African economy which threatens the very survival of African peoples as a race...

Thus, the European World's agelong policy of 'creeping' genocide against African peoples has, with its enhanced decapitalisation of the African economy in the past decade, been transformed into a policy of 'accelerated' genocide. The European World stands accused. If its so-called 'Africanists', the Olivers of its academy, have anything worthwhile in their scholarship to offer to outraged African peoples, it is to respond seriously to the legacy of this enduring genocide of the ages. When thirty years ago, Frantz Fanon, the influential African Caribbean national liberation theorist and philosopher wrote the following memorable lines, '[w]hen I search for Man in the technique and the style of Europe, I see only a succession of negations of man, and an avalanche of murders,'[68] there was some feeling of optimism among progressive peoples across the world, no doubt engendered by the celebrative mood of the imminent African liberation, that Europe's heinous crimes on Africans and other peoples in the previous 400 years would have ceased in the post-World War II epoch of the restoration of independence in the Southern World. Many now realise that that optimism was naive, if not foolish, as this has turned into the epoch of the European World 'accelerated' genocide on African peoples. Perhaps, the Olivers or 'Africanists' of the Western academy should also reflect in their deliberations on why the optimism of the world on this score has crashed so cruelly.

Alas, African (re)development presently is not geared towards achieving any other peoples' standards, including those even from Mars, Neptune, or far beyond! It is simply to survive an unrelenting holocaust of a millennium. It is in fact to ensure that Africans do not disappear as a people. And if this sounds apocalyptic, we only need recall that there were many peoples in the Americas, the Caribbean, and elsewhere who were obliterated by the West during the course of its conquest of the world in these past 500 years. At the rate that Africa is daily pumping out its wealth to feed the ever insatiable appetite of this rapacious Western World, the very basis of the survival of its peoples must be called to question.

Returning to the Source...

> Instead of presenting itself to history as an insolvent debtor, the Black World of the Egyptian is the very initiator of the 'western' civilization flaunted before our eyes today.

> - Cheikh Anta Diop

> You do not walk in, seize the land, the person, the history of another, and sit back and compose hymns of praise in his honour. To do that would amount to calling yourself a bandit; you don't want to do that. So what do you do? You construct very elaborate excuses for your action. You say, for instance, that the man in question is worthless and quite unfit to manage himself or his affairs. If there are valuable things like gold or diamonds which

you are carting away from his territory, you proceed to prove that he doesn't own them in the real sense of the word...

- Chinua Achebe

Earlier on this century, another European publicist writing on Africa who, no doubt, employed a variation from the standard theme of the horrid, the mystique, the unfathomable, the explorative, and thus the exploitable, that passes for the European World scholarship and publicity on Africa and its peoples (wherever they are), described Africa as an 'endless sea in which you can catch an infinite variety of fish.'[69] As if he was responding to this undisguised predatory preoccupation, the distinguished African American historian, Ivan Van Sertima, told a London conference in 1987 that Africa was more of a 'shattered diamond.' But even more importantly, Sertima emphasised, 'we are now putting the pieces together'[70] - a metaphor that encapsulates the autonomising confidence of Afrocentric scholarship.

Inevitably, African peoples had to begin to 'put (sic) these broken pieces together' *themselves*. It was important to seize the initiative, to dislodge European World scholarship on Africa (or what goes by the name 'African Studies' in the West) from the debilitating stranglehold that it had exercised on African existence since the beginning of the European conquest, but even more perniciously in its contemporary phase, which is generally classified under the rubric 'developing studies'. Thirty years earlier, 'modernisation studies'(then its baptismal name-switch, 'development studies', when the former concept became glaringly embarrassing even among its most fervent practitioners as it came under sustained attack from leading Southern World intellectuals for its gross a-historicity) initiated the ecstatic upsurge in the Western academy to study everything conceivable in the Africa 'emerging' from the throes of centuries of European conquest and pillage. Everything about Africa was to be studied, but this time given some 'modern' conceptual colouration in keeping with the *genre* of the epoch which was after all that of the restoration of independence for these peoples. Just a few years before, the same scholars now parading as modernisation/development 'experts' would have been teaching or researching in departments/faculties of anthropology or 'of primitive peoples/backward peoples/tribal peoples'. So, it was surely the proverbial disposition of the emperor changing his clothes, remaining the emperor nonetheless. The historiography of colonialism was conveniently re-fashioned to fit in with the vogue...

Everything about Africa was therefore to be studied. Everything: African ants, African lizards, African snakes, African lions, African hippos, African hogs, African goats, African chickens, African bees, African birds, African pasture, African mountains, African rivers, African gold, African diamonds, African petroleum, African coffee, African maize, African palmoil, African palmwine, African pound, African dollar, and of course, that most vilified subject (or rather object as these scholars would most probably prefer!) in Western scholarship on Africa, the African humanity -variously categorised as 'tribes', 'negroes', 'niggers', 'moors', 'blackermoors', 'blacks', 'blackies', 'darkies', 'bantus', 'guineas', 'hams', 'coons', 'wogs' 'coloured', 'colouring', 'people of colour', 'ethnics' or some other exotica. What is clear from any of these epithets of reference is that each simultaneously obliterates any meaningful, or easily discernible historical and geographical heritage of this humanity here on earth or indeed anywhere else in the planetary system, a crucial point to be elaborated further shortly.

Who are 'tribes'? What are 'tribes'? Where are 'tribes'?

Undoubtedly, 'tribe' is the most notoriously enduring of these racist labels of conquest that Europe has strapped onto the African identity and the one that Africans, both at home and the diaspora, who speak in any of the colonial languages that makes up the so-called official languages of business in Africa use willy-nilly whilst referring to other African peoples, and even to their *own* identity. Needless to state here that in no African language does there exist any term that approximates to this European concept of 'tribe', meaning 'non-people'. On the contrary, Africans, in their various languages, call other Africans by their designated name or just 'people' when a specific name is unknown.

In his new book on Africa entitled *The Black Man's Burden,* Basil Davidson, the British liberal historian whose scholarship on Africa was part of our earlier discussion of the 'British School of Colonial History', begins with an incisive reflection on the use of the concept 'tribe', as a description of African peoples that is evident in European imperial historiography, other related eurocentric scholarship, and generalised publicity on Africa. He observes that what the term does essentially is to attempt the denial, on the African historical scene, of the existence and ongoing development of societal institutions and processes very comparable to those in Europe (and elsewhere) on the eve of the outset of the European conquest. But this exercise of denial is of course a failure as Davidson notes: '"tribalism" (sic) has been used to express the solidarity and common loyalties of people who share among themselves a country and a culture. In this important sense, "tribalism" in Africa or elsewhere has "always" existed and has often been a force for good, a force creating a civil society dependent on laws and the rule of law. This meaning of "tribalism" is hard to distinguish in practice from the meaning of "nationalism."[as Europe uses in describing the European humanity's experience] Before the period of modern imperialism Europeans visiting and reporting Africa seldom drew any such distinctions...'[71]

So, contrary to the eurocentric summation on this important feature of African history, or as it would rather have it, 'Africa Without History', Davidson shows that what Europe calls 'tribes' in Africa are in fact 'nations' elsewhere. But this was not just an issue that rested merely on Europe's carefully calculated classificatory device aimed at laying the foundation in both its intellectual and 'popular' consciousness to justify its conquest and destruction of precolonial African development. There was something even more sinister that awaited Africa as this European 'reading' of the African historical process became incorporated in the ambience of Africa's 'post'-colonial societal development: 'Africans [must overcome this] atavistic tendency to live in "tribes" and to begin living in "nations." Much was written on the supposed miseries of the incorrigible "tribalism," and most of what was written, as may now be seen, completely missed the point. Not until years later, when a lot of damage had been done, was it understood that precolonial (sic) "tribalism" was no more peculiar to Africa than nineteenth century "nationalism" was to Europe.'[72] So, rather than utilise the ageless and priceless wealth of civilising histories encrusted in these African nations and peoples of pre-conquest African inheritance in the *reconstruction* of society following the restoration of independence, 'post'-colonial Africa, with the ever-energising prompting from Europe, continued the vilification and demonisation of (alas!) these only *surviving* heritage of 'Africaness' in the name of constructing a nation-state, *à la* Europe. But for these 'nation builders', the African nations of antiquity could not be relegated to the museums of inactivity, except of course they were destroyed. And before someone thinks that 'destroy' sounds emotive here, it is important to recall that six million Africans have been killed in the past 30 years, that is since the beginning of this era of the restoration of independence, in conflicts on the continent that have occurred specifically on whether or not African peoples wish to belong to one or the other of these 'nation-states'. This figure represents thrice as many number of Africans who lost their lives confronting 'classical' European colonialism, during the period, including confrontations in Kenya, Mozambique, Angola, Guinea-Bissau, Zimbabwe, Namibia and South Africa. In Nigeria, that quintessential flagship of the (British) 'nation- state' in Africa, 'nation builders' destroyed the lives of 2.5 million Africans in the eastern region of Biafra within a period of 30 months in the late 1960s in a war that was strategically directed by Britain and its coterie of allies from the Arab World and the former Soviet Union/East bloc states. We should also recall that this slaughtering was preceded and orchestrated in the initial massacre of 80,000 - 100,000 others between the months of May and September 1966 in northern Nigerian cities, towns and villages. In proportion, for instance, to the British population at the time, this grim casualty tally in Biafra would represent the death of 10 million Britons, a figure that is still far less than the total number of Britons killed during both World Wars I and II, the longer durations of the two latter conflicts notwithstanding. Even if on the Biafran experience alone, the 'curse of the nation-state' in relation to contemporary African existence is grim indeed.

Yet, thankfully, the overwhelming majority of Africans *still* do not live their every day normal lives as Senegalese, Nigerians, Zaireans, Kenyans, Chadians, Ruandans or whatever names these-disarticulated creatures of 'nation-states' call themselves. Instead, they live their lives as Wolof, Yoruba, Igbo, Ijo, Nupe, Bakongo, Baluba, Baganda, Kikuyu, Asante, Eritrean, Fante, Yergam, Ewe, and so on. Thirty years after Africa's 'post'-colonial restoration of independence, the principal sites of the continent's intellectual and cultural creativity remain located in the crucibles of these ancient nations and nationalities, and they will remain there forever. It is only during the process of the management of social production by these 'nation-states' that one can perhaps talk of an African living the life of a 'citizen' here. But in the African case as we have stressed throughout this study, this essentially means providing cheap and thus *easily dispensable* human labour for producing goods and services (primarily agricultural and mineralogical) for export to the West, and as the current situation desperately illustrates, it also incorporates the carrying of the burden of punishing social and economic deprivation as Africa continues to retain the unenviable accolade, for the 12th year in succession, of being a net exporter of capital to the West.

There are still outstanding points to be made on the European label of 'tribe' in describing the African humanity. If 'tribes' are really nothing less than 'nations', as Davidson argues in *Black Man's Burden*, we still need to know what European World publicists writing on African societies wish to convey when 'tribes' are 'tribes', rather than 'tribes' as 'nations'. Writing in 1990 in the London *New Statesman/Society* on the subject, E. Dumah notes: 'What constitutes a "tribe" (sic) defies precise definition; but as this word is generally used, it essentially means the social unit of anybody black living in Africa. Further distinctions of size (there are for example, around 15 million Nigerian Yoruba), language, music or cuisine are meaningless. Naturally, no serious British journalist [or/and academic] would ever call the Scots [about 5 million] or Welsh [about 1.5 million] a "tribe"... In being selectively applied to black people, "tribe" reveals its special pejorative quality.'[73] Besides its manifest racism, Dwumah reminds us of the consequences of the historical application of this term by Europe on the African heritage: 'to be designated a "tribe" by Europeans rendered any black community a potential target for invasion (and, occasionally, extermination).'[74]

So, what are 'tribes' *qua* 'tribes'? *They don't in fact exist in Africa, nor indeed anywhere else in the world*, except in the jaundiced mind of a European World desperate to cover up its murderous tracts after perpetrating the most horrific savagery of conquest ever recorded in human history. To this effect, while it is understandable, as in Davidson's excellent effort to demonstrate the comparable nature of European and African social institutions on this score (prior to Europe's invasion of Africa), despite the denial of 'official' Europe, there nonetheless remained a high probability that Europe would still have invented some demonised exotica to describe the African humanity even when it encountered superior social organisations and more humane civilisations in Africa (incidently, quite often the case) than what it had developed back home. This was because Europe could not openly acknowledge its debt to the strategic role that Africa, right from the Egyptian civilisation to the trans-Atlantic slave trade, played in its subsequent emergence as a global power after the 16th century AD *and*, at the same time, justify its criminal destruction of the African historical heritage. As novelist Chinua Achebe aptly puts it in the 1990 essay from which one of the epigraphs cited earlier on in this chapter is taken, 'If the worst comes to the worst, you may even be prepared to question whether such as he can be, like you, fully human. From denying the presence of a man standing there before you, you end up questioning his humanity... [I]n the colonial situation presence was the critical question, the critical word. Its denial was the keynote of colonialist ideology.'[75]

Restoration of Presence

Europe had to invent a 'tribe' of non-peoples in Africa *specifically* to deny the African presence after accomplishing its seizure of Africa. This is the key perspective of the African tragedy that Davidson's *Black Man's Burden* misses. This is why the text instead stretches itself unnecessarily to the limit to document 'parallel' European social structures/processes in Africa, on the eve of the invasion, to prove that Africa was also 'developing' just as Europe! For the Western academia, to which this book is principally directed (and which in the past has generally treated Davidson's writings on Africa with scant enthusiasm - ranging from polite containment to benign neglect, derision and even contempt as evident in some circles), there would now be very few who are not familiar with these facts of 'comparative' history. But even a growing number presently, on the eve of the year 2000, must know that the great arena of intellectual activity on this 'relation' is no longer the intensive quest to track down every European 'parallel' in African development but indeed the reverse: building up a dossier of European indebtedness to Africa ranging from the latter's philosophy, science, literature, jurisprudence, architecture and religion. On this accord, it is surprising that *The Black Man's Burden* is completely silent on the epochal scholarship of Cheikh Anta Diop and other Afrocentric historians who have worked strenuously in the past 45 years to reconstruct African history of the past 5000 years, namely since the Egyptian civilisation. And still on the issue of 'comparative' development (between Europe and Africa), Diop's *Precolonial Black Africa: A Comparative Study of the Political and Social System of Europe and Black Africa, from Antiquity to the Formation of Modern States*[76] is recommended as a much more illuminating and comprehensive text. If one were to examine, for example, the indices of the relative levels of social production, nature of organisation, treatment of peoples/nationalities/varying religions and beliefs, accumulation of surpluses, and the distribution of wealth, most of the African states/'nation-states' of the day far outstripped the records and standards of their European counterparts. These African social formations were not only superior to what Europe had to offer at the time, but their developments were dictated broadly by needs and priorities that were autochthonous. There could therefore be no question whatsoever for anyone to 'search for' European 'parallels' in these states. Such an enterprise would just not make any sense. The systematic destruction of this internal logic of African development soon after the European conquest got underway, crucial in the understanding of the contemporary African socio-economic crisis, is carefully documented in Water Rodney's classic, *How Europe Underdeveloped Africa* - a text not mentioned anywhere in the *Black Man's Burden.*

Basil Davidson concludes *Black Man's* Burden by calling for a new 'mode of politics of participation'[77] and decentralisation in Africa, aimed at the 'gradual dismantlement of the nation-state.'[78] This 'politics of participatory self-commitment' would 'raise a means of defending all those people who live now on the losing side of the existing world system, the poor and the very poor, and offer them a means of survival.'[79] Davidson already sees the 'evolution' of such a political process in contemporary Africa through the 'regional' organisations, ECOWAS (Economic Community of West African States) and SADECC (Southern African Development Coordination Conference). But both are curious examples of 'participatory' democracy to say the least! How the 'poor and the very poor' (in Africa) would hope to increase their level and range of 'participatory self-commitment' in organisations that merely serve as social clubs for mostly unelected and unelectable leaders whose existential obsession currently is to transfer as much African wealth that is possible year in, year out to the West, defies any logic of comprehension. But soon, on further reading, it becomes clearer why Davidson sees these 'regional' associations offering a route to this future of re-ordering of African societal democracy. These bodies, once again, represent some European 'parallel' on the African political landscape as Davidson is quick to remind everyone: '[I]f it is objected (as it often has been) that these are aims beyond realistic reach, because these are nation-states which will never accept a lessening of their sovereign powers and privileges, another confident answer is that such aims were already in process of being reached in that most unlikely of regions, Western Europe...'[80]

Davidson is right that the 'nation-state' in Africa is a bane on African progress, and, we should add, even more importantly, on the very survival of African peoples. The solution however does not lie in the creation of amorphous ensembles of further alienating structures of the ECOWASes of the European World which are at best (?) 'supranation-states'. No doubt, Basil Davidson arrives at this absurd conclusion essentially because *The Black Man's Burden* does not really critique the role of African human labour in these 'nation-states' (of Europe) dotted across Africa, treating it as inexorably given.

Towards Interiorisation

It should be stressed that the human resources of any given society constitute its engine of development. In Africa, these human resources have been trapped in an exogenously-oriented existence in the past one-half millennium, or since the outset of European imperialism. This presents an anomaly which many commentators, usually in the West, are often too keen to ignore: while most of Africa starves currently as a result of drastic short falls in domestic food production, there has however not been a corresponding decrease in Africa's production of the 'cash crops' and mineralogical products that the continent exports to the West. Conversely, the latter continue to be produced feverishly, creating the stockpile of overproduction which partly explains the general plummeting of the prices of these products that has been a distinct feature in Western commodity markets particularly in the last decade as we highlighted earlier on in this chapter. The *same* African labour which energetically, and unfailingly produces the export products for the West, is incapable of growing enough food to feed itself! Thus the tragedy of contemporary Africa cannot be exaggerated for it is a well-known fact that it is more of a taxing endeavour for human labour to grow tea or cocoa or rubber or cotton, or dig up a gold or diamond mine, than it is to grow yam or cocoyam or sweet potato, or melons or pumpkins or okro, or rear goats and sheep, or raise chickens and ducks. Added to this, of course, is that since 1981 Africa has been a net exporter of capital to the West, two-thirds of which represent the 'servicing' of the bogus debts which the West claims Africa owes it.

The future direction of Africa must therefore be fundamentally geared towards the interiorisation of the use of African human resource - a minimum requirement for the survival of the African race. This resource, the engine of societal development, will have to *disengage* from its present wasteful venture of working for the European World either in the mines or fields. Africa has to embark on a strategic retreat to its pre-colonial homelands of social formations to begin the arduous task of reconstructing a battered heritage. Essentially, this amounts to beginning all over again, from scratch, but with the objective of building up an economy, however rudimentary, *that has an internal logic and coherence to its existence*. For

Africa, it is indeed 'Morning Yet On Creation Day', to borrow from Africa's foremost novelist, author of the classic *Things Fall Apart* and one of the African World's most fervently and consistently optimistic writers. Africa has shown admirably throughout its history that it has a very resourceful human capability to direct the varying features of socio-economic activity on the continent, and elsewhere, including, alas, the entire epoch of the European conquest of the past 500 years when this has tragically meant working for the sustenance of the European World. The African human resource is therefore well equipped to spearhead the *autocentric* reconstruction envisaged here without any difficulties. Moreover, *all* African peoples, despite these centuries of displacements, dispossession and distortions, still retain the inner core of the spirituality of social existence which is communitarian - the human being exists as a purposive foundation block in a complex architectural web of relations which immanently links him or her to their community, itself part of a cosmogonical order, where the individual's needs are dictated by a holistic consideration of the religious ethos, the aesthetic and the ecological. In this dispensation, the individual's endless quest for material accumulation and the indefinite exploitation of societal resources, and/or those of others, to maintain material growth, as is known in virtually every philosophical thought system of social existence in the European World, is inconceivable. The latter *just does not* make sense in the African worldview. African peoples by and large have a more charitable, peaceable and optimistic disposition to life's mission than the European World where self-centredness, a suffocating pessimism and larcenous materialism have remained the norm. This is a pivotal facet of the point we made earlier that however intoxicated Western publicists get to feel about the material 'success' of the European World, the propelling motor of activity leading to that 'success' *only* makes sense within a cultural milieu, which would have worked out innumerable contentious issues that underpin the fundamental character of social existence. Development can therefore be nothing else but intrinsically tied up with *a* cultural environment.

Thus liberated from the shackles of the craggy chains of working for the European World in the 'nation-state' of contemporary Africa, the African human resource confronts the acute emergency that threatens its survival. African (re)development hence would no longer be predicated on the Western-created state as we have known it, which in any of its forms is conflictive, chauvinist, racist, hierarchical and hegemonic, as well as exploitative. As we have argued elsewhere,[81] this reorganisation of the use of African human resource expressly for domestic needs, goals and priorities requires an unmourned implosion of the existing 'nation-state(s)', leading to the provincialisation or decentralisation of socio-economic relations based on *real* Africa, the pre-colonial community of African nations, nationalities and principalities which, ironically, is that feature of the African civilisation most vilified in the racist discourses that pass for 'African Studies'/'African Reporting' in Western academia and media.

Both the West and the Arab/muslim World, as shown in chapter one of this book, have combined to force the subject of African (re)development in the current epoch to the very basic priorities of survival - to feed, to clothe, to house, to provide adequate health care, to provide security. These were needs which African peoples had achieved in full measure, *and taken for granted* in the various states and principalities that made up their civilisation which began 5000 years ago, at least 2000 years prior to the earliest meaningful evidence of pronounced civilisations of significant stature that was constructed by any peoples that would be part of the socio-cultural forebears of their present predators. It is clear that the African leadership, and indeed the contemporary African 'nation-state', that European invention which merely serves as a lever to transfer Africa's wealth to the West, *cannot* provide these fundamental needs of African peoples. But *real* Africa - Ewe, Vandau, Fante, Yoruba, Wolof, Kikuyu, Baule, Bakongo, Igbo, Hutu, and so on - *can* and *should* organise around these tasks, foremost of which is to convert, as of utmost necessity, every available farmland and garden in the community into the cultivation of food so that the people can obliterate the present starvation danger which threatens African survival. In effect, Africans should embark on creating an agricultural revolution in their homelends in this process of 're-inventing the wheel', dictated solely by their needs. They should then set up the order of priorities of the remainder of this survival venture as their various peoples deem fit, unlocking the creative energies therein to accomplish the tasks. African 'international' relations in the foreseeable future, diplomatic and economic, should focus on constructing an afrocentrically-rooted system of organisation sharing African skills and resources both at home and in the diaspora, for their *own* requirements. It will be a long, painful march of re-creativity, but out of this protracted process of (re)development will emerge the phoenix of African genius that set the pace of human creativity in antiquity.

Notes

1. Bill Weinberg, *War on the Land: Ecology and Politics in Central America* (London and New Jersey: Zed Books, 1991), p.162.
2. Ibid.
3. Ibid., p.163.
4. Oliver's article is not surprisingly captioned 'The condition of Africa,' *Times Literary Supplement* (London), 20 September 1991, in keeping with that Mazruiesque pathological imagery of Africa's historical process which excites the sensibilities of the so-called Africanists of the Western academy. For a discussion of the principal features of this imagery, see Herbert Ekwe-Ekwe, 'The antinomies of Ali Mazrui's worldview,' *West Africa* (London), 11 May 1987, pp.919-920.
5. Rodney, *How Europe Underdeveloped Africa*, op.cit. p.106.
6. Ibid.
7. Ibid.
8. Ibid.
9. Magdoff, *Imperialism*, op.cit., p.32.
10. Ibid., p.29.
11. Ibid.
12. Ibid.
13. Ibid., p.35.
14. Herbert Ekwe-Ekwe, *Conflict and Intervention in Africa* (London and Basingstoke: Macmillan, 1990), particularly ch 6.
15. Edited extract of Mark Tully, *No full stops in India* (London: Viking, 1991), published in *The Guardian* (London), 31 October 1991.
16. See 'Africa's Development Disaster,' *Comment* (London: Catholic Institute for International Affairs, 1985), p.19.
17. Ibid.
18. Frederick Clairmonte and John Cavanagh, 'Impossible debt on road to global ruin,' *The Guardian* (London), 9 January 1987.
19. Ibid.
20. John Clarke, *For richer, For Poorer: An Oxfam Report on Western Connections with World Hunger* (Oxford: Oxfam, 1986).
21. A.M. Babu, 'The Visionary Neto,' *African Events* (London), August 1988, p.32.
22. See *African Peoples Review* (Reading), June 1992, p.12.
23. Clairemonte and Cavanagh, op.cit.
24. See *The Challenge to the South: The Report of the South Commission*

(Oxford: Oxford University Press, 1990), pp.59-60.

25. Ibid.

26. *The Challenge to the South*, op.cit., p.229.

27. President Robert Mugabe (of Zimbabwe), *Financial Times* (London), 31 January 1989.

28. *The Challenge to the South*, op.cit.

29. Clairmonte and Cavanagh, op.cit.

30. See William Keeling, *Financial Times* (London), 27 June 1991 and 1 July 1991.

31. Chinua Achebe, *The Trouble with Nigeria* (Enugu: Fourth Dimension, 1983), p.9.

32. Herbert Ekwe-Ekwe, *Issues in Nigerian Politics Since the Fall of the Second Republic 1984-1990* (Lewiston/Queenston/Lampeter: Edwin Mellen, 1992).

33. Anthony Kirk-Greene and Douglas Rimmer, *Nigerian Since 1970: A Political and Economic Outline* (London: Hodder and Stoughton: 1981), p.84.

34. Toyin Falola and Julius Ihonvbere, *The Rise and Fall of Nigeria's Second Republic, 1979-1984* (London: Zed books, 1985), p.87. (Throughout most of the 1970s, the annual average US dollar exchange rate to the Nigerian naira was N1=$1.6.)

35. Ibid.

36. Ibid.

37. Ibid.

38. Ibid.

39. Kirk-Greene and Rimmer op.cit., p.142. See also R. Olufemi Ekundare, *An Economic History of Nigeria*, 1860-1960 (London: Methuen, 1973), pp.388-400.

40. Kirk-Greene and Rimmer, op.cit., p.142.

41. Billy Dudley, *An Introduction to Nigerian Government and Politics* (London and Basingstoke: 1982), p.226.

42. With acknowledgement to songwriter and journalist Onyeka Onwenu, for the title of her film, 'Nigeria: A squandering of Riches,' which focused on the gross mismanagement of the Nigerian economy during the Shagari presidency. The film was broadcast on BBC Television (London, 10 February 1984) as part of the 'The World About Us' series.

43. Ekundare, op.cit.; Dudley, op.cit., pp.232-234.

44. Bade Onimode, *Imperialism and Underdevelopment in Nigeria* (London: Zed Books, 1982), p.123.

45. Ibid., p.214 and pp.216-217, and Falola and Ihonvbere, op.cit., p.90.

46. Onimode, op.cit., p.214.

47. Ibid., p.216.

48. Ibid.

49. Falola and Ihonvbere, op.cit., pp.92-93.

50. *The Observer* (London), 22 January 1984.

51. For a graphic illustration of the endemic nature of corruption during the Shagari regime, see Chinua Achebe, op.cit., pp.37-43.

52. Edwin Madunagu, *Nigeria: The economy and the people - The political economy of state robbery and its popular democratic negation* (London: New Beacon Books, 1983) and the special edition devoted to the subject by *The Analyst* (Jos), Vol.2, No.3, 1987.

53. Tony Hawkins, *Financial Times* (London), 25 January 1985.

54. Ibid.

55. Charles Njoku, 'Illusion of Foreign Reserve,' *The African Guardian* (Lagos), 14 May 1990, p.7.

56. See 'Guide to the SFEM,' *West Africa* (London), 6 October 1986, pp.2091-2093.

57. John Ono, 'Nigeria: For "SFEM", Read "IMF",' *AfricAsia* (Paris), January 1987, p.24.

58. Ibid.

59. Njoku, op.cit.

60. 'Nigerians buy more,' *Export Times* (London), November 1987.

61. *West Africa* (London), 10 August 1987, p.1552.

62. Ibid.

63. *The Times* (London), 1 August 1989.

64. Alexander Cockburn, 'Scenes from an inferno,' *New Statesman & Society* (London), 12 May 1989, p.15.

65. Oliver, op.cit., p.9.

66. David Dabydeen, 'This land is our land,' *New Statesman &Society* (London), 1 November 1991, p.19.

67. Quoted in Marshall Frady, 'The Life and Legacy of Malcolm X,' *The Sunday Times Magazine* (London), 14 February 1993, p.16.

68. Frantz Fanon, *Wretched of the Earth* (Harmondsworth: Penguin Books, 1978), p.252.

69. Quoted by Ifi Amadiume, 'African Political Systems and Culture: From Before Columbus to the Twentieth Century,' (*mimeo*,nd.), p.2.

70. Ibid.

71. Basil Davidson, *Black Man's Burden: Africa and the Curse of the Nation-State* (London: James Currey, 1992), p.11.

72. Ibid., p.75.

73. E. Dumah, 'Imperialist language,' *The New Statesman & Society* (London), 5 October 1990, p.24.

74. Ibid.

75. Chinua Achebe, 'African Literature as restoration of Celebration,' *Kunapipi* (Aarhus), Vol XII, No.2, 1990, p.4.

76. (New York: Lawrence Hill Books, 1987).

77. Davidson, op.cit., p.320.

78. Ibid., p.321.

79. Ibid.

80. Ibid., p.322.

81. Herbert Ekwe-Ekwe, *The Biafra War, Nigeria and the Aftermath* (Lewiston/Queenston/Lampeter: Edwin Mellen, 1990)

Select Bibliography

Achebe, Chinua, *Morning Yet on Creation Day* (London: Heinemann Education Books, 1977).

Achebe, Chinua, *The Trouble with Nigeria* (Enugu: Fourth Dimension, 1983).

Achebe, Chinua, 'African Literature as restoration of Celebration,' *Kunapipi* (Aarhus), Vol XII, No.2, 1990.

African Peoples Review (Reading), June 1992.

'Africa's Development Disaster,' *Comment* (London: Catholic Institute for International Affairs, 1985).

Ake, Claude, *A Political Economy of Africa* (Harlow: Longman, 1981).

Amadiume, Ifi, *Afrikan Matriarchal Foundations: The Igbo Case* (London: Karnak House,1987).

Amadiume, Ifi, *Male Daughters, Female Husbands: Gender and Sex in an African Society* (London: Zed Books, 1987).

Anonymous, *Independent Kenya* (London: Zed, 1982).

Babu, A.M., 'The Visionary Neto,' *African Events* (London), August 1988.

Beaud, Michel, *A History of Capitalism: 1500-1980* (New York: Monthly Review, 1983).

Boahen, A. Adu, ed., *Unesco General History of Africa: Vol. VII - Africa under Colonial Domination 1800-1935* (Paris/London: Unesco and Heinemann Education Books, 1985).

Chinweizu, *The West and the Rest of Us* (New York: Random House, 1975).

Chinweizu, *Decolonising the African Mind* (Lagos: Pero, 1987).

Chinweizu, 'Cries for Freedom,' *The Times Higher Education Supplement* (London), 17 February 1989

Chomsky, Noam, 'The United States: From Greece to El Salvador, in Chomsky, *et al, Superpowers in Collision* (Harmondsworth: Penguin Books, 1982).

Chomsky, Noam, 'Intervention in Vietnam and Central America: Parallels and Differences,' *Monthly Review*, Vol 37, No.4, September 1985.

Clairmonte, Frederick, and John Cavanagh, 'Impossible debt on   road to global ruin,' *The Guardian* (London), 9 January 1987.

Clarke, John, *For Richer, For Poorer: An Oxfam Report on Western Connections with World Hunger* (Oxford: Oxfam, 1986).

Cockburn, Alexander, 'Scenes from an inferno,' *New Statesman &   Society* (London), 12 May 1989.

Davidson, Basil, *Africa in History* (London: Paladin Books,1978).

Davidson, Basil, *Black Man's Burden: Africa and the Curse of the   Nation-State* (London: James Currey, 1992).

Diop, Cheikh Anta, *The African Origin of Civilisation: Myth or   Reality* (Westport: Lawrence Hill Books, 1974).

Dike, K. Onwuka, *Trade and Politics in the Niger Delta* (Oxford: Oxfrod University Press, 1956).

Diop, Cheikh Anta, *Precolonial Black Africa: A Comparative Study   of the Political and Social Systems of Europe and Black Africa, from Antiquity to the Formation of Modern States* (New York: Lawrence Hill Books, 1987)

Diop, Cheikh Anta, *Civilisation or Barbarism* (New York: Lawrence Hill Books, 1991).

Dudley, Billy, *An Introduction to Nigerian Government and Politics* (London and Basingstoke: 1982).

Dumah, E., 'Imperialist language,' *The New Statesman & Society* (London), 5 October 1990.

Ekundare, R. Olufemi, *An Economic History of Nigeria: 1860-1960* (London: Methuen, 1973).

Ekwe-Ekwe, Herbert, 'South Africa: The agony of Thatcherism,' *The Guardian* (Lagos), 27 July 1986.

Ekwe-Ekwe, Herbert, 'The antinomies of Ali Mazrui's worldview,' *West Africa* (London), 11 May 1987.

Ekwe-Ekwe, Herbert, *Conflict and Intervention in Africa* (London and Basingstoke: Macmillan, 1990).

Ekwe-Ekwe, Herbert, *The Biafra War, Nigeria and the Aftermath* (Lewiston/Queenston/Lampeter: Edwin Mellen, 1990).

Ekwe-Ekwe, Herbert, *Issues in Nigerian Politics Since the Fall of the Second Republic 1984-1990* (Lewiston/Queenston/Lampeter: Edwin Mellen, 1992).

Falola, Toyin and Julius Ihonvbere, *The Rise and Fall of Nigeria's Second Republic, 1979-1984* (London: Zed Books, 1985).

Fanon, Frantz, *Wretched of the Earth* (Harmondsworth: Penguin Books, 1978).

Fitch, Bob and Mary Oppenheimer, *Ghana: End of an Illusion* (New York and London: Monthly Review, 1966).

Flynn, Laurie, *Studded with Diamonds and paved with Gold: Miners, Mining companies and Human Rights in Southern Africa* (London: Bloomsbury, 1992).

Fryer, Peter, *Black People in the British Empire* (London: Pluto, 1989).

Hill, Christopher, 'Lies about crimes,' *The Guardian* (London), 29 May 1989.

James, C.L.R., *Nkrumah and the Ghana Revolution* (London: Alison and Busby, 1982).

Madunagu, Edwin, *Nigeria: The economy and the people - The political economy of state robbery and its popular democratic negation* (London: New Beacon Books, 1983).

Magdoff, Harry, *Imperialism: From the Colonial Age to the Present* (New York and London: Monthly Review, 1978).

Mao Tse-Tung, 'On contradiction,' in Mao Tse-Tung, *Five Essays on Philosophy* (Peking: Foreign Language Press, 1977).

Mokhtar, G., ed., *General History of Africa VOL. II: Ancient Civilisations of Africa* (Paris/London: Unesco and Heinemann Educational Books, 1985).

Morrison, Toni, Interview, 'Living Memory,' *City Limits* (London), 31 March-7 April 1988.

National Security Council Interdisciplinary Group for Africa, Study in Response to National Security Study Memorandum 39: Southern Africa. AF/NSC-1969, 15 August 1969, in Mohamed A. El Khawas and Barry Cohen (ed.), *The Kissinger Study of Southern Africa: National Security Memorandum 39* (Westport, Connecticut: Lawrence Hill, 1976).

Niane, D.T., in Niane, ed., *Unesco General History of Africa: VOL.IV - Africa From the Twelfth to Sixteenth Century* (Paris/London: Unesco and Heinemann Education Books, 1984).

Njoku, Charles, 'Illusion of Foreign Reserve,' *The African Guardian* (Lagos), 14 May 1990.

Nnoli, Okwudiba, 'A Short History of Nigerian Underdevelopment,' in Nnoli, ed., *Path to Nigerian Development* (Dakar: Codesria, 1981).

Nwabara, S.N., *Iboland: A Century of Contact with Britain 1860 - 1960* (London: Hodder and Stoughton, 1977).

Ohadike, D.C., 'Exploitation of Labour: Waged and Forced,' in Toyin Falola ed., *Britain and Nigeria: Exploitation or Development?* (London and New Jersey: Zed Books, 1987).

Okoye, Mokwugo, *Embattled Men: Profiles in Social Adjustment* (Enugu: Fourth Dimension, 1980).

Oliver, Roland, 'The condition of Africa,' *Times Literary Supplement* (London), 20 September 1991.

Onimode, Bade, *Imperialism and Underdevelopment in Nigeria: The Dialectics of Mass Poverty* (London: Zed Books, 1982).

Ono, John, 'Nigeria: For "SFEM", Read "IMF",' *AfricAsia* (Paris), January 1987.

Rodney, Walter, *How Europe Underdeveloped Africa* (London:Bogle-L'Ouverture, 1972).

Rodney, Walter, 'The African Revolution,' in Paul Buhle, ed.,*C.L.R. James: His Life and Work* (London/New York: Alison & Busby, 1986).

Seidmann, Ann, and Neva Seidmann Makgetla, *Outposts of Monopoly Capitalism: Southern Africa in the Changing Global Economy*

(Westport/London: Lawrence Hill and Zed, 1980).

Spady, James G., 'The Changing Perception of C.A. Diop and his Work: The Preeminence of a Scientific Spirit,' in Ivan Van Sertima, ed., *Great African Thinkers, Vol.1: Cheikh Anta Diop* (New Brunswick & Oxford: Transaction Books, 1986).

Tarikh (Lagos), Vol.4, Nos 3 and 4, 1973.

The Analyst (Jos), Vol.2, No.3, 1987.

The Challenge to the South: The Report of the South Commission Oxford: Oxford University Press, 1990).

Tully, Mark, *No Full Stops in India* (London: Viking, 1991).

Vercruijsse, Emile, *The Penetration of Capitalism: A West African Case Study* (London and The Hague: Zed Books/Institute of Social Studies: 1984).

Wallerstein, Immanuel, 'The Three Stages of African Involvement in the World-Economy,' in Peter Gutkind and Immanuel Wallerstein, eds., *The Political Economy of Contemporary Africa* (California and London: Sage, 1976).

Weinberg, Bill, *War on the Land: Ecology and Politics in Central America* (London and New Jersey: Zed Books, 1991).

Williams, Eric, *Capitalism and Slavery* (London: Andre Deutsch, 1972).

Williams, Chancellor, *The Destruction of the Black Civilisation* (Chicago: Third World, 1987).

Index

Achebe, Chinua, 64n.8, 75, 80, 92, 96, 103n.31, 104n.51, 105n.75

Africa, African World: arable land potential, 73-74; 'Burden Prize for Western Wealth', 76; capital transfer, net capital transfer from, 2-3, 53 *passim*; central/east Africa, 4-5, 18-19, 30, 33; economy, 'cash crop'/export product, 11ff; economy, disarticulated, 4-7 *passim*; foundations of Afrocentrism, 58 *passim*; holocaust, 5-6 *passim*; independence, re-establishment of independence, restoration of independence, 1, 27-37, 45ff; matriarchal, matriarchal system, 3; 'non'-state, anti-state states, 3; neo-colonialism, 48 *passim*; north Africa, 1, 32, 82; pan-African liberation congresses, 35-36, 37; population, population density, 70-72; 'post'-colonial conflicts and wars, 72-73, 94-95; resistance to aggression, 7-11, 27-37; resources, human and natural, 5-6; scholars, 2; 'seasons' of conquest, 1-7; southern Africa, 15, 18, 19-22, 24, 30, 57-58; towards provincialised civilisations, 99-101; west Africa, 1-4, 8, 29, 30, 32

Africa and History (Davidson), 23, 24

Ake, Claude, 39n.38, 40n.48, 42n.106, 64n.19

Algeria, 47, 48, 50, 84

Almond, Gabriel, 54

Almoravids, 1

Amadiume, Ifi, 3, 38n.13, 38n.14, 38n.15, 104n.69

Americas, North and South, 6, 33, 72, 74; Latin America, 50, 54, 71, 74, 78

Angola, 7, 46, 50, 54, 57-58, 95

Arab, Arabia, Arab World, Arabisation, 1-4, 9, 18-19, 82, 87, 101; conquest of parts of Africa, 1-5, 9-10, 59, 72; de-Africanisation as conquest, 1-5; *see also* Africa

Asante, 10, 11, 95

Asia, 1, 4, 18-19, 25, 32, 33, 35-37, 48, 71; Asiatic, Asiatic patriarchy, 4; Euro-Asian patriarchy, 3; Indo-European World, 3

Askia Mohammed, 3, 9

Atlantic Ocean, 1, 74

Australasia, 25

Austria-Hungary, 28

Babangida, Ibrahim, 85-87

Babu, A.M., 102n.21

Baganda, 95

Bahro, Rudolf, 70

Bakongo, 95

Baluba, 95

Bambara, 10

Baro, 8

Baule, 10, 101

Beaud, Michel, 6; 39n.27

Belgium, 6, 13, 26, 50; Leopold II (king) of, 15-16, 26; atrocities in Africa, 15-16, 23

Beloved (Morrison), 62

Bemba, 10

Benin, 10

Bihe, 10

Biafra, 50; Biafra War, 81, 83, 95

Binder, Leonard, 54

Birmingham, 2